Madison County Kentucky Court Order Book A 1787-1791

Jackie Couture

HERITAGE BOOKS
2006

HERITAGE BOOKS
AN IMPRINT OF HERITAGE BOOKS, INC.

Books, CDs, and more—Worldwide

For our listing of thousands of titles see our website at
www.HeritageBooks.com

Published 2006 by
HERITAGE BOOKS, INC.
Publishing Division
65 East Main Street
Westminster, Maryland 21157-5026

Copyright © 1996 Jackie Couture

Other books by the author:
Madison County, Kentucky Court Order Book B, 1791-1801

All rights reserved. No part of this book may be reproduced or transmitted in any form or by any means, electronic or mechanical, including photocopying, recording or by any information storage and retrieval system without written permission from the author, except for the inclusion of brief quotations in a review.

International Standard Book Number: 978-0-7884-0594-2

Introduction

This order book covers the time period from 1787 to 1791. At this time Madison County included all of present-day Clay, Jackson, and Owsley Counties and parts of Breathitt, Estill, Garrard, Lee, Leslie, and Rockcastle Counties.

I started transcribing this book from microfilm and found that many pages were illegible. When I went to the courthouse to check the original, I found, much to my dismay, that the book in the courthouse was different from the book I was transcribing. Information was basically the same, but there were more details in this version. Upon further investigation I found that what I was transcribing was the Minute Book that was used to take notes while Court was in session. The Minute Book is full of abbreviations; it lists no first names on court cases, and it mentions wives simply as "ux." The Order Book in the vault room at the courthouse is a clerk's copy of the Minute Book which is locked in the safe.

There are items in each version that do not appear in the other; therefore, I felt that I should include both versions in this book. This abstract is based on the Minute Book. Anything that appears in the Order Book, but not the Minute Book is in italics. All abbreviations have been spelled out when possible. The spelling in the original Minute Book has not been corrected. Punctuation, however, has been added for easier reading and to clarify sentences.

There are several items concerning deeds that need clarification. If the seller appears in court to acknowledge that he is indeed selling the property in question, then there are no witnesses. If the seller does not appear in person, the deed is proved by one or more witnesses (usually three). If all witnesses appear to prove the deed, it is ordered recorded. However, if all witnesses do not appear in court, the deed is ordered certified until such time as the other witnesses appear or the seller appears in person to acknowledge the deed. At this time the deed is recorded.

The cases from 1787 to 1803 have been rearranged alphabetically by Plaintiff rather than the box and bundle numbers originally used. All cases after 1803 still use the box and bundle system. A glossary is included to explain some of the legal terms used in the order book. The index is an every-name index except for the justices of the peace. They were indexed when they took the oath of office but not on succeeding court days. Subjects were also indexed with the exception of roads.

The lawsuits mentioned in this Order Book can be found at the Kentucky Department for Libraries and Archives, 300 Coffee Tree Road, Frankfort, KY 40602-0537.

> Jackie Couture
> August 1996

Acknowledgements

I would like to give thanks to the staff at Special Collections and Archives at Eastern Kentucky University Library for their help with this project. Thanks also to Anne Crabb for her advice and knowledge of the early history of Madison County. Special thanks to my husband who put up with many late suppers and a messy house while I sat in front of the computer and microfilm reader for hours.

At the House of George **Adams**, Gent. in Madison County on Tuesday the 22nd of August one thousand seven hundred and eighty six.

Present George **Adams**, John **Snody**, Christopher **Irvine**, David **Guest**, James **Barnet**, John **Bowels**, Archibald **Woods**, Sr. Nicholas **George**, Joseph **Kennedy**, Gentlemen.

A commission of the Peace and of Oyer and Terminer directed to the said George **Adams**, John **Snoddy**, Christopher **Irvine**, David **Guest** [*Gass*], James **Barnet**, John **Bowles**, James **Thomson**, Archibald **Woods**, Nicholas **George**, and Joseph **Kennedy**, Gent. Constituting and appointing the Justices of the Peace and of Oyer and Terminer for the said County of Madison. Whereupon John **Snoddy** and Christopher **Irvine**, gent., administered the Oath of Fidelity to the commonwealth and also the oath of a Justice of the Peace as the Law directs to the said George **Adams** and then the said oaths were severally administered to John **Snoddy**, Christopher **Irvine**, David **Guest**, James **Barnet**, John **Bowles**, Archibald **Woods**, Nicholas **George**, and Joseph **Kennedy** by George **Adams**, Gent. and thereupon a court was held for the said County of Madison.

Present the Justices first mentioned.

Joseph **Kennedy**, gent., produced a commission from his Excellency the Governor appointing him sheriff of this County which being read and thereupon the said Joseph **Kennedy** took the Oath of Fidelity to the commonwealth and the Oath of Office and together with John **Logan**, Christopher **Irvine**, and Thomas **Kennedy** his securities entered into Bond for the faithful performance of his office conditioned as the Law directs.

The Court doth appoint William **Irvine** to be Clerk of this Court whereupon he entered into Bond and Security as the Law directs and also took the Oath of Fidelity to the commonwealth and the Oath of Office. *Securities were Harry **Innes** and Christopher **Irvine**.*

James **Barnett**, Esqr. produced a commission from his Excellency the Governor appointing him Lieutenant of this County whereupon he took the Oath of Fidelity to the commonwealth and the Oath of Office.

Thomas **Kennedy**, Esqr. produced a commission from his Excellency the Governor appointing him Lieutenant Colonel in the Militia of this County whereupon he took the Oath of Fidelity to the commonwealth and the Oath of Office.

Madison County, Kentucky Court Order Book A

On the Motion of John **Anderson** his ear mark being swollow fork in each ear is Ordered to be recorded.

On the motion of Samuel **Rice** his ear mark bees a crop and a hole in the right ear and a crop and under keel in the left is Ordered to be recorded.

The Court is adjourned til tomorrow ten o'clock.

George Adams

At a Court continued and held for Madison County at house of George **Adams**, gent August the 23, 1786.

Present George **Adams**, John **Snoddy**, Christopher **Irvine**, David **Gass**, James **Barnet**, John **Boyle**, Archibald **Woods** and Nicholas **George**, gent.

Ordered that Addam **Woods**, Jacob **Sternes**, Hickison **Grubbs**, Samuel **Estill**, Bennett **Pempberton** and Joseph **Kennedy** be recommended to his Excellency the Governor as proper persons to be commissioned as Captains in the Militia of this County.

*Ordered that Charles **Cavenaugh**, Jesse **Hodges**, William **Ham**, Gerrard **Hume**, Mathew **Scott** and Peter **Woods** be recommended to His Excellency the Governor as proper persons to be Commissioned as Lieutenants of the Militia in this County.*

Ordered that James **Barry**, Samuel **South**, Oswell **Towns**, William **Bartlet**, Joseph **Ray** and William **Morrison** be recommended to his Excellency the Governor as proper persons to be commissioned as Ensigns in the Militia in this County.

Absent James **Barnet**, gent.

Ordered James **Robertson** [*Robinson*], Thomas **Warren**, Aquila **White**, Ambrose **Coffe**, Richard **Singleton**, William **Hollan** be appointed Constables in this County.

On motion of Joseph **Kennedy**, gent. Robert **Branks** is appointed his Deputy in this County whereupon he took oath prescribed by Law.

Ordered that the Court be Adjourned til tomorrow ten o'clock.

George **Adams**

At a Court continued and held for Madison County at the house of George **Adams**, gent. August the 24th one thousand seven hundred and eighty six.

Madison County, Kentucky Court Order Book A 3

Present George **Adams**, John **Snody**, Christopher **Irvine**, David **Gass**, James **Barnet**, John **Boyls**, Archibald **Woods** and Nicholas **George**, gent.

Ordered that Samuel **Woods**, gent. be recommended to his Excellency the Governor as proper person to be commissioned as Coroner in this County.

Ordered that John **Boyls**, gent. be Recommended to his Excellency the Governor as proper person to commission as Major in Militia in this County.

On the Motion of James **Robertson** [*Robinson*] Letters of administration is granted him on the personal estate of James **McNealy** Deceased. *Security is Joseph Scott.*

Ordered that James **Adams**, Humphrey **Best**, Samuel **Woods**, Alexander **Denny** or any three of them being first sworn do apppraise the estate of James **McNealy** Deceased.

James **French** and James **Anderson** applied to this Court to be Nominated as principal Surveyor for this County the Court being devided in sentiment they refer the matter to the President & Master of William and Mary University

Ordered that the Court be Adjourned until tomorrow twelve o'clock.

George **Adams**

At a Court continued and held for Madison County at the house of George **Adams**, gent Augt 25th 1786.

Present George **Adams**, John **Snoddy**, John **Boyles**, Archibald **Woods**, gent.

On motion of Green **Clay** his ear mark a crop and slight in the left ear and two slight in the right ear is ordered to be recorded.

On Motion of Thomas **Kennedy** his ear mark a crop in the right ear and a hole in the same is Ordered to be recorded.

On Motion of Thomas **Kennedy** his brand is 96 on the left side of the ribs is Ordered to be recorded.

On motion of John **Boyles** his ear mark a crop of the left ear a slight under the keel in the right ear is Ordered to be recorded.

On motion of Archibald **Woods** his ear mark a crop and under keel in each ear is Ordered to be recorded.

On the motion of Richard **Reynolds** his ear mark a crop in each ear and under keel in the right ear is Ordered to be recorded.

On the motion of Alexander **Reed** his ear mark a crop and two slights in the right ear and under in the left ear is Ordered to be recorded.

On motion of Samuel **Gordon** his ear mark a slight in each ear and under keel in the right ear is Ordered to be recorded.

Ordered the Court adjourned from this place to the house of David **Gass** until Court in Course.

George **Adams**

At a Court held for Madison County at the house of David **Gass**, gent. on Tuesday the 24th of October 1786.

Present George **Adams**, David **Gass**, James **Barnett**, John **Boyle** and Archibald **Woods**, gent.

Ordered that John **Snoddy** and Nicholas **George**, gent be summoned to appear at the next court to be held for this County to shew cause why they do not attend to the duties of their offices.

A deed from John **Tanner** to Archibald **Woods** proved by the oath of Samuel **Estill** and John **South** and ordered to be certified.

Ordered that George **Boon**, Robert **Roads**, Higgason **Grubbs**, John **Turner** or any three of them being first sworn do review the most convenient for a road from Irvines Lick to the Mouth of Tates Creek and report the same.

Ordered that Green **Clay**, Robert **Roads**, William **Ham** and William **Holland** or any three of them do review a way for a Road from the house of John **Woodruff** to **Ham's** Mill and report the same they being first sworn.

Ordered that John **Doty** be appointed Surveyor of the road from Lincoln Courthouse to Paint Lick beginning County line thence on to Thomas **Tiptons** and John **Boyles**, Gent be appointed to lay of the thith for labor on said road.

Ordered that Thomas **Tipton** be appointed Surveyor of the Road from his house to Paint Lick and that John **Boyles**, gent do lott the tiths to work on said road.

Ordered that Samuel **Gordon** be appointed Surveyor of the road leading from Crab Orchard to Paint Lick from the County line to where it intersects the road from Lincoln Courthouse and John **Boyles** appointed.

Ordered that Joseph **Scott** be appointed Surveyor of the road from Paint Lick to Silver Creek and that George **Adams,** gent be appointed to lott the tiths to work on the said road.

Ordered that Edmond **Terrel** be appointed Surveyor of the road from the county line leeding from Danville to the road leeding from Lincoln Courthouse and John **Boyles** be appointed to lott of the tiths for the same.

Ordered that James **Hendrix,** David **Cruse,** John **White** and James **Martin** do review a way for a road from the mouth of Tates Creek to intersect the road leeding from Boonesborough to Paint Lick and report the same.

Aaron **Lewis** his ear mark a smooth crop in the left ear and swallow fork in the right ear is Ordered to be recorded.

On motion of David **Gass** his ear mark a smooth crop of the right ear is Ordered to be recorded.

On the motion of James **Stephenson** his ear mark a crop and a hole in the right and a crop and slit in the left Ordered to be recorded. Also his brand JS one across the other.

Ordered that the south end of this house be appointed the jail of this County until next court.

Joseph **Kennedy** Sheriff came into court and complained of the insufficiency of the jail.

Ordered that the Court be adjourned untill Court in Course.

George Adams

At a Court held for the County of Madison at the house of David **Gass** on Tuesday the 25th day of Dec 1786.

Present George **Adams,** John **Snoddy,** David **Gass,** James **Barnett** and Archibald **Woods,** gent.

On motion of James **Davis** it is ordered that Thomas **Gass** and Richard **Barrow** be summoned to appear at next court.

On motion of Michael **McNealy** letters of Administration are granted him on the estate of Charles **Chafray,** deceased. *Securities are Matthew Scott and John Anderson.* Ordered that James **Robertson,** James **Adams,** Samuel **Woods** and William **Miller** or any three of them being first sworn do proceed to appraise the estate of Charles **Chafray** and make return thereof to next court.

Elizabeth **Stephenson** vs. James **Stephenson** dismissed.

James **French** produced a commission from his Excellency the Governour appointing him Surveyor of this County whereupon he made oath. Executed and acknowledged bond as the Law directs. *Securities are Archibald **Woods** and John **Miller**.*

Ordered that the Surveyor of this County extend the County line between this County and Lincoln in conjunction with the Surveyor of Lincoln as soon as conveniency will admit.

John **Snoddy**, gent. produced a commission from his Excellency the Governour of Colonel in the Militia and took the oath as prescribed by Law.

Joseph **Kennedy**, gent. produced a Commission from his Excellency the governor appointing him Captain in the militia and took the oath prescribed by law.

Mathew **Scot**, gent. produced a commission from his Excellency the Governour appointing him a Lieutenant of the Militia and took oaths prescribed by Law.

Ordered that Charles **Cavanaugh**, gent. be appointed Captain in the Militia.

Ordered that James **Berry**, gent. Lieutenant and Thomas **Turner**, gent. Ensign to Captain **Kavanaugh**.

Ordered that Samuel **Rice**, gent. be appointed Lieutenant in Captain **Pembertons** Company.

On motion of Lidia **Irvine**, William **Irvine** and Hail **Talbert** Letters of Administration is granted them on the Estate of Christopher **Irvine** deceased whereupon they made oath executed and acknowledged Bond as the law directs. *Securities are Archibald **Woods**, John **Miller** and Joseph **Kennedy**.*

Ordered that John **Woods**, James **French**, Thomas **Shelton** and Adam **Woods** or any three of them being first sworn do proceed to appraise the estate of Christopher **Irvine** deceased and make return to the Court.

The persons appointed to view a way for a road from the mouth of Tates Creek to Irvine Lick made report. Ordered that the same be established agreeable to said report.

Ordered that George **Boone** be appointed surveyor of the road from the mouth of Tates Creek to William **Williams** and that Archibald **Woods**, gent. be appointed to allot the tithes.

Madison County, Kentucky Court Order Book A

Ordered that Robert **Roads** be appointed surveyor of the road from William **Williams** to where it intersects the road from Boonesborough and to set up a post *with directions at the forks of the said roads*. Archibald **Woods**, gent. to allot the tithes.

On motion of the Reverend James **Haw** who produced his credentials he is permitted to solemnize matromony.

The persons appointed to view a way for a road from the mouth of Jacks Creek to intersect the road leading from Boonesborough to Paint Lick made report and the same is established.

Ordered that David **Crews** be appointed surveyor of the road from Jacks Creek. Archibald **Woods**, gent. appointed to allot the tithes.

Ordered that William **Orear** be appointed surveyor of the road from Boonesborough to **Woodrooffs**. Archibald **Woods**, gent. to allot the tithes.

A deed from John **Tanner** to Archibald **Woods** further proved by the oath of James **French**.

Ordered that James **Hendricks** be appointed surveyor of the road from **Woodrooff's** to Irvines Lick and that Archibald **Woods**, gent. allot the tithes.

Ordered that the Court be adjourned till Court in course.

George **Adams**

At a Court held for Madison County at the house of David **Gass**, gent. on Tuesday the 27th of February 1787.

Present George **Adams**, John **Snody**, David **Gass**, James **Barnett**, John **Boyles** and Archibald **Woods**, gent.

Samuel **Woods**, Esqr. produced a commission from his Excellency appointing him Coroner in this County whereupon he took the oath prescribed by Law.

Ordered that George **Adams**, gent. be appointed to take a list of tiths and taxable property in the bounds of Captain **Kennedy's** company.

Ordered John **Boyles**, gent. be appointed to take list of tithes and taxable property in the bounds of Captain **Pemperton's** Company.

Ordered John **Snoddy**, gent. be appointed to take the list of tiths and taxable property in bounds Captain **Estill's** Company.

Ordered that David **Gass**, gent. be appointed to take the tithes and taxable property in the bounds of Captain **Kavanaugh** Company.

Ordered that James **Barnett**, gent. be appointed to take the list of tiths and taxable property in bounds of Captain **Stearns** Company.

Ordered that Archibald **Woods**, gent. be appointed to take the list of tiths and taxable property in the bounds of Captain **Grubb's** Company.

Ordered that Micheal **McNealy**, Green **Clay**, and Thomas **Kennedy** be appointed commissioners of land tax in this county.

Jesse **Wilson**[*Watson*] who was bound by Recognizance to appear here today to answer the Complaint of Elizabeth **Stephenson** for a breach of the peace. Who appeared accordingly the parties being fully heard it is the oppinion of the Court that said **Wilson** be discharged.

James **Stephenson** who was bound by Recognizance to appear today to answer the complaint of Elizabeth **Stephenson** is continued.

On Motion of David **Gass** it is ordered that Thomas **Warren** and Susanah **Hanon** be summoned to appear at the next court.

A deed George **Smith** to William **McGuire** proved by the oath of Thomas **McGuire** is to be certifyed.

A deed from *Charles* **Campbell** to *Absolom* **Brown** acknowledged and Ordered to be recorded.

A deed from *Samuel* **Davis** to *David* **Gass** acknowledged and ordered to be recorded.

A report of a road from **Ham's** Mill to **Woodroff** was returned and it is Ordered to be establish so far as will intersect the road from the mouth of Tates Creek and Irvine's Lick.

Ordered that William **Ham** be appointed surveyor of the road from **Ham's** Mill to intersect the road from Tates Creek to Irvines Lick and Archibald **Woods**, gent. is appointed to lott of the tiths to work on the same.

Ordered that the Church Wardens of this County bind James **Campbell** son to Prudence **Piper** [*Peppers*] to Thomas **McGuire**.

Bent **Pemberton** and Jacob **Stearns** produced commissions from his Excellency appointing them Captains in the Militia in the County whereupon they took the oaths prescribed by Law.

Peter **Woods** and Jesse **Hoges** produced commissions from his Excellency appointing them Lieutenant in the Militia of this County whereupon they took the oaths prescribed by Law.

William **Morrison** [*Moore*], Samuel **South**, William **Bartlet** produced commissions from his Excellency appointing them Ensigns in the Militia of this County whereupon they took the oaths prescribed by Law.

Ordered that John **Miller**, Thomas **Shelton**, Stephen **Hancock** and Haile **Talbot** be appointed to view a way for a road from the mouth of Jack Creek to intersect the road from Boonesborough to Paint Lick and report to the County.

On the motion of Charles **Kavanaugh** his ear mark a crop in the right ear and a hole in the left is Ordered to be recorded.

On motion of Charles **Kavanaugh**, Junr. his ear mark a crop and a slit in the right a crop and under keel in the left is Ordered to be recorded.

On the motion to Hugh **Campbell** his ear mark a crop and under keel in the left and under keel in the right is Ordered to be recorded.

On motion of Robert **Roads** his ear mark a crop and under Keel in each ear is Ordered to be recorded.

On motion of Dennis **Burgin** his ear mark a slit and under keel in each ear is Ordered to be recorded.

On motion of William **Turpin** his ear mark a sowlow fork in the left and a half crop in the right is Ordered to be recorded.

On motion of Samuel **Woods** his ear mark a crop in the right and a half crop in the left is Ordered to be recorded.

Ordered that the place for the Court house of this County to be built at or near where Captain **Gass**' path leaves the Great Road at Taylors Fork.

George **Adams**, gent. enters his objection to the above order as a place not proper for want of the necessary article water.

Ordered that the Court be adjourned until tomorrow nine o'clock.

George **Adams**

At a Court held for Madison County at the house of David **Gass**, gent. on Wednesday the 28th day of February 1787.

Present John **Snody**, David **Gass**, James **Barnett**, John **Boyle** and Archibald **Woods**, gent.

Ordered that the Court house for this County be built agreeable to a plan filed in the clerks office.

Ordered that George **Adams**, James **Barnett**, John **Snody** and Archibald **Woods**, gents. be appointed commission for to direct the public buildings in this county.

On the motion of Thomas **Kennedy** Ordered that James **Stephenson** and Joshua **Abner** be summon to appear at the next court.

Ordered that James **Anderson**, James **Barnett** and John **Holley** be appointed to examine Hugh **Ross** suveyor and certify the same to Court.

Present George **Adams**, gent.

On motion of Adam **Woods** his ear mark a half crop in the right and a slit in the left is Ordered to be recorded.

Ordered that George **Adams**, gent. be appointed to purchase books for the Clerks Jury office and to purchase on credit if in his power.

Hugh **Ross** who was nominated by James **French** as one of his deputies produced a certificate from the examined that he is qualified for the same whereupon you took the oaths prescribed by law.

A deed from *Jacob* **Stearns** and *Elizabeth his wife* to *John* **Holley** acknowledged and Ordered to be recorded.

On motion of John **Carpenter** his ear mark a sowlow fork in the left ear and a hole in the right is Ordered to be recorded.

On the motion of Thomas **Warren** his ear mark a crop and a hole in the right and a crop and a slit in the left is Ordered to be recorded.

On the motion of John **Holley** his ear mark a crop and slit in the left and under keel in the right is Ordered to be recorded.

Ordered that George **Adams**, gent. be appointed to provide a house for the Court to set in next month at the place appointed for fixing this Courthouse and that the Court pay for the said house.

Ordered that Archibald **Woods** and David **Gass**, gents be appointed to lay off the place for the foregone house.

On motion of Christopher **Owley** Letters of Administration is granted him on the estate of John **Owley** deceased whereupon he executed bond and took the oath prescribed by Law. *Security is George* ***Adams***.

Ordered that John **Boyles**, Thomas **Kennedy**, Samuel **Rice** and John **Doty** be appointed to appraise the estate of John **Owley** deceased.

Ordered that Aaron **Lewis**, Robert **Roads**, Moses **Dowley**, Bent **Pemberton** and John **Miller** be recommended to his excellency as a proper persons to be added to the commission of the peace in this County.

Madison County, Kentucky Court Order Book A   11

Ordered that the Court Adjourn until Court in Course.

George **Adams**

At a Court called and held at the house of David **Gass**, gent. the 7th day of March 1787 for examination of James **McManas** charged with feloniously buggering a mare before the worshipful. John **Snody**, David **Gass**, John **Boyles** and Archibald **Woods**, gents.

The prisoner being led to the Barr and being demanded of him whether he was guilty of the charge aforesaid or not says he is not guilty whereupon sundry witnesses were sworn and examined and the prisoner heard in his defense on consideration whereof it is the opinion of the Court that the said James shall be discharged and acquited.

The Court is disolved.

John **Snoddy**

At a Court of Quarter Sessions held for Madison County at the house of David **Gass**, gent. on Tuesday the 7th of March 1787.

Present George **Adams**, John **Snoddy**, David **Gass**, John **Boyles** and Archibald **Woods**, gents.

Michael **McNeely** foreman; John **Anderson**, Thomas **Kennedy**, John **Maxfield**, Andrew **Kennedy**, Robert **Henderson**, Humphrey **Best**, Ambrose **Ross**, Stephen **Handcock**, William **Handcock**, James **Crofford**, Henry **Owley**, Lofty **Pullins**, Edward **Stephenson**, William **Morrison**, Boud **Estill**, Peter **Taylor**, Green **Clay** were sworn a grandjury for this County having received their charge went out to consider there presentments.

John **Holder** vs. Rubin **Proctor** Continued.
Same vs. Talbot **Arther** Continued.
Same vs. Zachriah **Dozer** Continued.
Benjamin **Woodard** vs. Hugh **Ross** Continued.
John **Logan** vs. David **Lynch** judgement confest for debt and costs. *Defendant did not appear so ruled for the Plaintiff £ 1-14.*
Richard **Masterson** vs. Hugh **Ross** continued.
James **Robertson** vs. Thomas **Maxfield** judgement for debt and cost. *Defendant did not appear so ruled for the Plaintiff £ 2-2.*

David **Hogen** vs. John **Cortney** judgment for £ 1-5 and cost. *Defendant did not appear so ruled for the Plaintiff.*

William **Young** vs. Solomon **Brendage** judgment for five pounds and costs. *Defendant did not appear so ruled for the Plaintiff.*

John **Cloin** vs. John **McMahan** continued.

Philip **Bush** vs. John **McMahan** continued.

Ordered that James **Barnett** and James **Anderson** do examine Jonathan **Longstreth** as a Deputy Surveyor and Certify the same to the court.

Rates of Liquor in this County
Rum per gal 15/
Whiskey per gal 8/
Dinner 1/3
Breakfast . . . . s-1[*1/1*]
Lodging . . . . /6
Pasturage of hay or fodder for 24 hrs . . . . /6
Corn per pottel . . . . /4

Ordered that the Several Ordinary Keepers in this County do Charge and receive in their Respective Ordinarys agreeable to the foregoing rates.

A report of a road from the mouth of Jacks Creek to intersect the Road from Boonesborough to Paint Lick was returned and is established agreeable to said report Ordered to be recorded.

Jonathan **Longsteth** who was nominated by James **French** as one of his deputies produced a certificate from the examiner that he is capable of Executing the said office whereupon he took the oath prescribed by Law.

Ordered that James **Anderson** and John **Adams** be appointed to examine William **Calk** and William **Orear** as Deputy Surveyor and Certified the same to the court.

Ordered that James **Anderson** and John **Adams** be appointed to examine Caleb **Smith** as a Deputy Surveyor and certify the same.

A deed from Flanders **Callaway** to David **Cruse** was proved by oaths of Abraham **Newland**, Archibald **Bell**, and Elijah **Cruse** and Ordered to be recorded.

Christopher **Owley** is appointed Guardian to Rebeka **Owley** orphan of John **Owley** deceased whereupon entered into Bond conditioned as the Law directs. *Security is James Stephenson.*

A deed from David **Cruse** to Abraham **Newland** was acknowledged and Ordered to be recorded.

A deed from David **Cruse** to Jeremiah **Cruse** was acknowledged and Ordered to be recorded.

Ordered that the persons presented by the Grandjury be summoned to appear at the next Court Quarter Session to be held for this County.

On the motion of James **Mason** his ear mark a crop and slit and under keel in the right ear and a crop and a slit in the left is Ordered to be recorded.

On the motion of Edward **Stephenson** his ear mark an under keel in the right ear and a hole in the left is ordered to be recorded.

Present James **Barnett**, gent.

On the motion of Andrew **Boggey** his ear mark a crop and slit in the right ear is Ordered to be recorded.

On motion of Thomas **Kennedy** it ordered that Joshua **Abner** be removed from the house of James **Stephenson** unto Thomas **Kennedy's** and there remain until the next Court and that he *Stephenson and Abner* be summoned to appear at the next court.

*William **Orear** and William **Calk*** Surveyor in this County who produced a Certifycate by James **French** deputy from the Examinators that they are capable to execute the said office whereupon they took the oath prescribed by Law.

William **Morrison** vs. Richard **Singleton** judgment confessed for debt and costs.

Ordered that James **Barnett** and Archibald **Woods**, gent. be appointed to assess the lands as commissioners of the land tax in this county.

Samuel **Campbell** his ear mark a crop and slit in the left ear is Ordered to be recorded.

Ordered the Court adjourned from this place to the house prepared for a protempro Courthouse and until Court in Course.

George **Adams**

At a court held at Madison Courthouse on Tuesday the 24th day of April 1787.

Present George **Adams**, David **Gass**, James **Barnett**, John **Boyles** and Archibald **Woods**, gent.

A deed from Higgason **Grubbs** and *Lucy* to Edward **Turner** was acknowledged and Ordered to be recorded. fem relinquished and Ordered to be recorded.

Same to Samuel **Freeman** same Ordered to be recorded.

A Deed from William **Hoy** to John **Miller** was acknowledged and Ordered to be recorded.

The Court doth adjourn untill tomorrow 8 o'clock.

George **Adams**

Wednesday the 25th day of April 1787

Present George **Adams**, John **Snoddy**, David **Gass**, John **Boyles** and Archibald **Woods**, gent. Absent George **Adams**.

George **Adams** and Michael **McNeely** is appointed guardians to Jam and David **McNeely** orphans of James **McNeely** deceased whereupon they executed Bond as the Law directs. *Security is Archibald **Woods**.*

An inventory and appraisment of the estate of Charles **Caffery** deceased was returned and Ordered to be recorded.

Thomas **Hall** and Thomas **Todd**, esqr. produced a license to practice as attorneys in the County Courts took the oaths prescribed by Law.

Thomas **Hall**, Esqr. recommended to the Attorney General for this district as a proper person to be commissioned as a Deputy State Attorney in this County.

Present James **Barnett**, gent.

Ordered that Wednesday succeeding the fourth Tuesday in every month be appointed a Rule a day in this County.

Ordered that George **Miller**, Moses **Doley**, William **Hopkins** and John **Mounts** be appointed to view a way for a road from the mouth of Sugar Creek to Thomas **Banks**.

Benjamin **Woodard** vs. Hugh **Ross** Discontinued.

John **Holder** vs. Talbot **Arther** dismissed.

Same vs. Rubin **Proctor** Judgment for £ 1-15 and costs. *Defendant did not appear so ruled for the Plaintiff.*

Same vs. Zachariah **Dozer** dismissed.

Ordered that the Sheriff summon Aquila **White** and his wife to appear at next court to answer the complaint of Lydia **Bone** for a breach of the Peace.

Richard **Masterson** vs. Hugh **Ross** judgment for debt and costs. *Defendant did not appear so ruled for the Plaintiff £ 2-9.*

Philip **Bush** vs. John **McMahan** on attatchment judgment for £ 7-4-6 and Ordered of sale. *Sheriff levied attachment on 80 bushels of corn and one ax. Ordered to sell attached goods to settle debt.*

Ordered that Haill **Talbot** be appointed surveyor of the road from William **Hancocks** to the Courthouse and Archibald **Woods**, gent. appointed to lot of the tiths to work.

Ordered that Peter **Woods** be appointed surveyor of the road from Archibald **Woods** to the foard of Taylors Fork and Archibald **Woods**, gent. appointed to lot of the tithes to work on the same.

Ordered that Joshua **Abner** be continued at Thomas **Kennedy's** until next Court and that he be summoned to appear here at the same.

Ordered that Charles **Debrell** and Robert **Roads** be recommended to his Excellency as proper persons to be commissioned as Captain in the Militia of this County.

Ordered that Ralph **Morgan** and John **Phelps** be recommended to his Excellency as proper persons to be Commissioned as Lieutenant in the Militia in this County.

Ordered that John **Sanders** and John **Tuder** be recommended to his Excellency as proper persons to be commissioned as Ensign in the Militia in this County.

Ordered that Ozewell **Townson** be recommended as a Lieutenant and James **Hendrix** as an Ensign in Captain **Grubbs** Company.

Ordered that Hugh **Campbell** and John **Campbell** is allowed five pounds ten schillings for building a Courthouse and to be paid out of the first Collection that may be made in the County.

James **Smith** vs. Aquila **White**, Higgason **Grubbs** and Charles **Kavanaugh** Special Bail.

Ordered that the Court be adjourned untill Court in Course.

George **Adams**

At a Court of Quarter Sessions held at Madison Courthouse on Tuesday the 22nd of May 1787.

Present George **Adams**, John **Snoddy**, David **Gass**, James **Barnett**, John **Boyles** and Archibald **Woods**, gent.

John **Miller**, foreman; John **Anderson**, Thomas **Kennedy**, Andrew **Kennedy**, James **Crafford**, Ambrose **Ross**, Green **Clay**, William **Hancock**, Stephen **Hancock**, Humphrey **Best**, William **Morrison**, Zach **Dozer**, Boud **Estill**, Loft **Pulin**, David **Maxfield** [*Maxwell*] and John **Holley** were sworn a Grandjury for this County having received their charge Retired to consider on there presentments.

A deed from George **Adams** to Thimothy **Logan** was acknowledged and Ordered to be recorded.

Ordered that William **Morrison**, Stephen **Merrit**, David **Maxfield**, Mose **Dolly** be appointed to view a way for a road from near Joseph **Ray's** unto the Courthouse.

A report of a road from the mouth of Sugar Creek to or near Thomas **Bankes** was returned and Ordered established agreeable to said report and Ordered to be recorded.

Ordered that William **Anderson**, John **Gass**, Isaac **Anderson** and James **Stephenson** be appointed to view a way for a road from the Foard on Silver Creek to the Courthouse.

A deed from William **Hoy** to William **Purkins** was proved by the oath of Absolom **Crook** and Andrew **Bogey** was Ordered to be certifyed.

The Grandjury returned and made the following presentments. We of the Grandjury do present the Surveyor of the road from Irvine's Lick *to the Courthouse* for not keep the same in repair.

A deed from William **Hoy** to Zach **Dozer** was proven by the oath of James **French** and Absolom **Crook** and Ordered to be certifyed.

A deed from William **Hoy** to John **White** was proved by the oath of Absolom **Crook** and Ordered to be certifyed.

Ordered that the Sherif do summon a Jury of twelve men to ascertain the damages done by William **Ham's** mill dam to the land of Philip **Williams** and to value one acre and report to next court.

Ordered that William **Ham**, William **McGuire**, Hugh **Campbell**, John **Sanders** be appointed to view a way for a road from the mouth of Silver Creek to this place.

A deed from John **Tanner** to Absolom **Crook** was proved by the oath of John **White** and Ordered to be certifyed.

Ordered that John **Clark** be appointed Surveyor of the road from the mouth of Sugar Creek to Thomas **Banks** and John **Boyles** is appointed to Lott of the tithes.

Deed and Comm from William **Hoy** and *Sarah his wife* to John **Sapaton** was acknowledged and Ordered to be recorded.

A deed from John **Tanner** to Charles **Ballew** was proved by the oath of Absolom **Crook** and Ordered to be certifyed.

William **Irvine** his ear mark a crop and a slit in the right ear and a half crop in the left is Ordered to be recorded.

Lydia **Irvine** her ear mark a crop in the left ear and a half crop in the right is Ordered to be recorded.

On the motion of William **Orear** his ear mark swoler fork over keel in the right a crop and a crop under keel in the left is Ordered to be recorded.

On the motion of John **Sapaton** his ear mark a swooler fork in each ear is Ordered to be recorded.

On the motion of John **Kincade** his ear mark a crop and a slit in the left ear and a half ponney out of the upper said of the right is Ordered to be recorded.

John **Doty** his ear mark a crop and a slit and under keel in the left a crop and a slit in the right on under keel is Ordered to be recorded.

John **Allen**, Esqr. produced a licence to practice as an attorney whereupon he is permitted to practice as the same in this Court and he took the oaths prescribed by Law.

David **Hogen** who was bound by Recognizance to appear here to answer the complaint of John **Dyer** for feloniously stealing his horse who appeared accordingly and the Court is of the opinion that the said **Hogen** be discharged as no person appeared to prosecute.

John **Smith** vs. Ralph **Morgan** continued.
John **Cline** vs. Baptis **Clark** continued.
Eli **Cleveland** vs. Jesse **Hoges** dismissed
James **Baisley** vs. John **Gordon** continued.

Walter **Beall** vs. Z. **Dozier** continued.
Same vs. So. **Brundrige** continued.
Andrew **Beall** vs. Same

Ordered that Michael **McNeely**, John **Miller** and Andrew **Kennedy** be appointed Commission of the taxes in this County.

John **Cortney** vs. William **Glenn** judgment for £ 8 and summon Hugh **Ross** as garneshee.

Certifycate from the Clerk of Burk County to Robert **Brank**, *Senr. certifying that he was exempted from paying County Levy* was produced in Court and Ordered to be recorded.

Ordered that Michael **Owley** be appointed Constable in this County.

Ordered that Daniel **Williams** be appointed Constable in this County.

Ordered an Inventory and Appraisement of James **McNeely** deceased estate was returned and Ordered to be recorded.

Ordered that the Court be adjourned untill Court in course.

George **Adams**

At a Court held at Madison Courthouse on Tuesday the 26th day of June 1787.

Present George **Adams**, John **Snoddy**, David **Gass**, John **Boyles** and Archibald **Woods**, gent.

Robert **Roads** and John **Miller**, gent. took the oath of fidelity and of Justices of the peace and of Oyer and Terminer whereupon they are appointed to the said office.

Present John **Miller**, gent.

Joseph **Ray**, Esqr. produced a commission from his Excellency appointing him an Ensign in the Militia whereupon he took the oaths prescribed by Law.

James **Barnett**, gent. returned a Certificate that Andrew **Kennedy** had taken the oath of a Commissioner and the said certificate is Ordered to be recorded.

An agreement between William **Hoy** and James **French** was proved by the oath of Absolem **Crook** and Ordered to be recorded.

Jury that was summoned to ascertain the damage done by William **Ham's** Mill to the land of Philip **Williams** made report and the said report is Ordered to be recorded.

Charles **Dibrell** produced a commission from his Excellency the Governor appointed him Captain in the Militia in this County whereupon he took the oaths prescribed by Law.

John **Saders** [*Sanders*] produced a commission from his Excellency appointing him Ensign in the Millitia in this County and he took the oath prescribed by Law.

A deed and Comm from *William* **Hoy** and *Sarah his wife* to Leonard **Heatherly** acknowledged and Ordered to be recorded.

A deed from Joseph and Andrew **Kennedy** to Humphrey **Best** was acknowledged and Ordered to be recorded.

Walter **Beall** vs. Zach **Dozer** judgment £ 2-9. *Defendant did not appear so ruled for the Plaintiff.*

Same vs. Solomon **Brundaeg** judgment for £ 2-16-4p. *Defendant did not appear so ruled for the Plaintiff.*

Andrew **Beall** vs Same judgment £ 4-5-0 with interest from March the 20th 1787. *Defendant did not appear so ruled for the Plaintiff.*

John **Bazely** vs *John* **Gorden** dismissed.

John **Cline** vs *Baptist* **Clark** dismissed.

John **Smith** vs Ralph **Morgan** judgment £ 4-2-9. *Defendant did not appear so ruled for the Plaintiff.*

John **Campbell** his ear an over keel in each ear is Ordered to be recorded.

Ordered that an amendment be made to an Order of the last Court for appointing Commissioners as follows that Michael **McNeely** executed the said office in the bound of Captain **Kennedy** and Captain **Pemberton** Companys and John **Miller** in the bounds of Captain **Estill** and Captain **Kavanaugh's** Company and Andrew **Kennedy** in the bounds of Captain **Grubbs** and **Stearns** Companys.

Present Robert **Roads**, gent.

Samuel **Rice** produced a Commission from his Excellency appointing him Lieutenant in the Militia in this County and he took the oaths prescribed by Law.

John **Boyle**, Esqr. produced a Commission from his Excellency appointing him Major in the Militia in this County whereupon he took the oaths prescribed by Law.

A report of a road from the mouth of Silver Creek to the Courthouse was returned and the said report is establish and Ordered to be recorded.

Ordered that William **Turpin** be appointed Surveyor of the road from the mouth of Silver Creek to Bound **Estill** and R. **Roads** [*David Gass*], gent. is appointed to lott of the tithes to work on the same.

Ordered that Hugh **Campbell** be appointed surveyor of the road from Boud **Estill's** to the Courthouse and David **Gass**, gent. is appointed to lot of the tithes to work on the same.

On the motion of Joseph **Titus** his ear mark a crop of the right ear and an under keel in each is Ordered to be recorded.

Ordered that Court be adjourned untill Court in Course.

George **Adams**

At A Court held for Madison County at the Courthouse the 24th day of July 1787.

Present George **Adams**, John **Snoddy**, David **Gass**, James **Barnett**, John **Boyles**, Archibald **Woods**, Robert **Rhodes** and John **Miller**, gent.

Aron **Lewis** and Moses **Doley** come in to Court and took the Oath of Fidelity of Justices of the Peace and of Oyer and Terminer and took the Oaths.

Absent Archibald **Woods** and Aron **Lewis**, gent.

A deed from Thomas **Barton** to William **Hoy** and John **South** was proved by the oath of Aron **Lewis** and Archibald **Woods** and Ordered to be certified.

Present Archibald **Woods** and Aron **Lewis**, gent.

A deed from Peter **Taylor** and *Ann his wife* to William **Briscoe** fem privately examined and Ordered to be recorded.

Archibald **Clinton** is appointed guardian to Hanah **Amdam** [*Adams*] and Robert **Adams** *orphans of James Adams deceased* whereupon he entered into bond conditions as the Law directs. *Securities are Alexander* **Denny** *and Thomas* **Kennedy**.

Absent James **Barnett**, gent.

An inventory and appraisment of the estate of John **Wooly** [*Owley*] was returned and Ordered to be recorded.

Ordered that John **Burton** alias **Hardwick** be continued with Abraham **Barton** until a further order of this Court.

A Power of Attorney from Boud **Estill** to Thomas **Hugvet** was acknowledged and Ordered to be recorded.

Absent Aron **Lewis**, gent.

Ordered that Hugh **Ross** and James **Anderson** be appointed to examin Aron **Lewis** as a deputy surveyor and make report to the Court.

A list of Surveys was returned by the Surveyor of this County and Ordered to be recorded.

Ordered that Samuel **Estill**, James **Anderson**, Isaac **Anderson**, and Edward **Stephenson** be appointed to view a way for a road from the Round Stone Lick to this Courthouse and make report to the next Court.

Aron **Lewis** who was nominated by James **French** as one of his deputies produced a certificate from the examiners that he is capable to execute the said office whereupon he took the oath prescribed by Law.

Ordered that Joseph **Kennedy** and George **Adams**, gent. be recommended to his Excellency as proper persons to be commissioned as Sheriff of this County.

Ordered that John **Wilson** be recommended to his Excellency as a proper person to be commissioned as Ensign in the Militia in this County.

Ordered that the Clerk and Surveyor be appointed to purchase books such as ar necessary for their respective offices.

Ordered that the Court be adjourned until Court in Course.

George **Adams**

At a Court of Quarter Session held at Madison Courthouse on Tuesday the 28th August 1787.

Present George **Adams**, John **Snoddy**, James **Barnett**, Archibald **Woods**, gent. Present Robert **Rodes**, John **Miller**, gent.

Ordered that Haile **Talbot** be appointed Lieutenant in the Militia in this County whereupon he took the oaths prescribed by Law.

Present David **Gass**.

Robert **Henderson**, Foreman; Thomas **Kennedy**, James **Crafford**, Andrew **Kennedy**, John **Maxwell**, John **Sapington**, Samuel **Estill**, Ambrose **Ross**, Humphrey **Best**, Boud **Estill**, Stephen **Handcock**, William **Hancock**, Henry **Woley** [*Owley*], Peter **Woley** [*Owley*], Zach **Dozer**, William **Briscoe**, John **Anderson**, Thimoby **Logan** and William **Morrison** were sworn a Grand Jury for this County having received there charge retired to Consider of there presentments.

An instrument of writing from Ebenezer S. **Platt** to John **Holly** and John **Wilkinson** was proved by oath of Francis **Holly** and Ordered to be recorded.

Present Moses **Doley**, gent.

The persons appointed to view a way for a road from the Round Stone Lick to the Courthouse made report which is established and Ordered to be recorded.

Absent James **Barnett**, gent.

The grandjury returned and made the following presentments.

Peter **Taylor** for getting drunk and for profane swearing.

A deed from George **Adams** to Richard **Walker** was acknowledged and Ordered to be recorded.

A certificate of the oaths of John **Miller** and Andrew **Kennedy** as Commissioners was returned and Ordered to be recorded.

Ordered that James **Black** be appointed surveyor of the road from the Courthouse to the foard on Silver Creek leeding to the Hazel Patch and David **Gass**, gent. to a lott the tiths to work the same.

Absent David **Gass**, gent.

Ordered that James **Anderson** be appointed surveyor of the road from the foard on Silver Creek to Edward **Stephenson** and John **Snoddy**, gent. be appointed to Lott of the tiths to work on the same.

A deposition of Ambrose **Ross** was returned into Court and Ordered to be recorded.

Ordered that William **Crafford** is appointed surveyor of the road from Edward **Stephenson's** to the Round Stone Lick. John **Boyles**, gent. be appointed to lott of the tithes to work on the same.

Present David **Gass**, gent.

William **Morrison** appointed surveyor of the road from Paint Lick to Silver Creek in the Room of Joseph **Scott** and the same hands is to work under him.

Madison County, Kentucky Court Order Book A   23

Ordered that a certifycate be granted Michael **McNeely** for twenty days service as Commissioner in this County.

Ordered that John **Lane** be exempted from paying County Leavy.

Ordered that the Court be adjourned until tomorrow 10 o'clock.

George **Adams**

Wednesday the 29th day of August 1787

Present David **Gass**, James **Barnett**, Archibald **Woods** and John **Miller**, gent.

A certificate of the oath of Michael **McNeely** as a Commissioner was returned and Ordered to be recorded.

James **McManus** vs John **Owens** dismissed.

William **Robinson** assee of Benjamin **Grason** vs Green **Clay** judgment according to note. £ 2-9 and costs. *Defendant did not appear so ruled for the Plaintiff.*

William **Griffin** vs James **Dozer** judgment per note. £ 4 and costs. *Defendant did not appear so ruled for the Plaintiff.*

John **Pattie** vs John **Vivion** discontinued.

Thomas **Brown** vs Hugh **Ross** continued.

John **McClure** vs James **Mason** continued.

James **Davis** assee vs Samuel **Harris** and John **Harris** judgment for £ 1-15-8 with interest. *Defendant did not appear so ruled for the Plaintiff.*

Ambrose **Ross** vs Baptist **Clark** dismissed.

On the Motion of Robert **Henderson** Cor **Daugherty** to be summoned to appear at the next Court to shew cause why his ill treatment to his Daugherty Isable and it is Ordered that Judy **Taril**, Edmund **Terrel**, David **Maxwell**, Mary **Maxwell**, Stephen **Merrit**, Marget **Merrit**, Robert **Hill**, Thomas **Tipton**, Joseph **Paton**, Joseph **Ray** and John **Cline** be summed to testify the same.

A report of road from the Courthouse to intersct the Danville Road below Thomas **Leavingston** was returned which was established and Ordered to be recorded.

Ordered that Stephen **Merrit** be appointed surveyor of the said road and George **Adams** to alott the tithes to work on the same.

Ordered that William **Anderson**, Isaac **Anderson**, John **Gass** and James **Stephenson** be appointed to view the most convenient and best way for a road from the foard on Silver Creek to the Courthouse.

Ordered that the Court be adjourned Untill Court in Course.

David **Gass**

At a Court held at Madison Courthouse on Tuesday the 25th of September 1787.

Present George **Adams**, David **Gass**, Archibald **Woods**, Robert **Roads** and John **Miller**, gent.

On motion of Archibald **Woods** and Thomas **Shelton** letters of administration is granted them on the estate of Ph **Kavanaugh** deceased also they are appointed guardians to William and Ann **Kavanaugh** the orphans of the said **Kavanaugh** and they entered into bond conditioned as the Law directs. *Securities are Samuel Estill and James Black.*

Ordered that John **Miller**, Haile **Talbot**, James **French** and Stephen **Hancock** be appointed to appraise the estate of Philimon **Kavanaugh**, deceased.

Ordered that Edmond **Terrel**, James **Fennel**, William **Finnel** and Cornelius **Daugherty** be appointed to view a road from the top of the hill on the north*east* side of the Paint Lick to where it may intersect the Danville Road.

John **Leverige** who was bound be recognizance to answer the complaint of Patrick **Galahar** for a breach of peace personally appeared and the Court is of the oppinion that the said **Leveridge** is guilty the Sheriff is Ordered to take him in custody.

John **Miller** came into Court and made oath that he had served nine days as a Commisssioner and a certificate is ordered him accordingly.

Ordered that Joseph **Titus** be admited to build a mill on Taylors Fork of Silver Creek on his own land.

On the motion of William **Irvine**, Haile **Talbot** and Thomas **Reynolds** is admited to qualify as his deputies protempro.

William **Irvine** Clerk of this Court took the oaths prescribed by Law.

Present James **Barnett**, gent.

Ordered that Cornelius **Daugherty's** daughter Issabell be set at liberty and no longer under his jurisdiction and that she be summons to appear at the next December court in order to choose a guardian also that she remain under Michael **McNeely's** directions untill the same.

On the motion of Robert **Henderson** his ear mark an under keel in the right ear is Ordered to be recorded.

The report of a road from the ford of Silver Creek to the Courthouse intersecting the road to the Round Stone Lick is established and ordered to be recorded.

Ordered that Thomas **Campbell** is appointed surveyor of the said road and David **Gass** be appointed to lott of the tithes to work the same.

Ordered that John **Pitman** be appointed surveyor of the road from the top of the hill N.E. side of Paint Lick to intersect the road from Silver Creek to the Courthouse.

Thomas **Brown** vs Hugh **Ross** judgment for three pounds six shillings and nine pence.

Ordered that James **Barnett** be appointed to lot of the tiths to work under John **Pitman** as surveyor of a road.

Ordered that James **Henderson** be appointed surveyor of the road in the room of Thomas **Tipton**.

The Court called on the Sheriff to give security for the collection of the Revenue and he informd the Court that he used his utmost endeavours but could get no person to undertake as security.

Ordered that the Court be adjourned till Court in Course.

George **Adams**

At a Court held for Madison County on Tuesday 23rd of Oct. 1787.

Present George **Adams**, David **Gass**, Archibald **Woods** and John **Miller**, gent.

A deed from John **Ellis** to Aron **King** was proved by the oath of James **Crossgrove**, Baptist **Clark**, and Moses **McHughs** and Ordered to be recorded.

Ordered that James **Barnett**, John **Boyles**, Alexander **Reed** and Alexander **Denny** or any three of them be appointed to settle the Accouts of

James **Robertson** administrator of James **McNealy**, deceased and make report at the December Court next.

A deed of gift of negroe name **Jacob** from Robert **Burton** to Allen **Burton** was proved by the oath of John **Phelps**, Junr. and Abraham **Burton** and Ordered Recorded.

Ordered that Archibald **Woods** administrator of Phileman **Kavanaugh** deceased pay unto Thomas **Shelton** thirty seven pounds twelve shillings and six pence for his disbursements for the use of and taking care of two orphan children of the said decedent and twelve pounds seven shilling and six pence for raising and taking care of the stock and other things belonging to the said decendants estate for the space of six years and six months.

Ordered that Peter **Hacket**, Nicholas **Proctor**, John **Carpenter** and James **Black** do view a road the best and nearest way from **Estill's** Station to the Courthouse and make report thereof to the next December Court.

A report of a road leading from the top of the hill on the north east side of Paint Lick to where it intersects the Danville Road on the top of the hill on the north east side of Back Creek was returned and that summonses issue to those persons through whose land the said road runs as mentioned in the said report.

Ordered that the Court be adjourned untill the next Court.

George **Adams**

At a Court held for Madison County on Tuesday 27th of November 1787.

Present George **Adams**, John **Snoddy**, James **Barnett**, John **Boyle**, Archibald **Woods**, Aron **Lewis**, Moses **Dooly**, gent.

Michael **McNeely**, foreman; John **Anderson**, James **Crafford**, Andrew **Kennedy**, Peter **Owley**, Henry **Owley**, William **Robinson** [*Robertson*], Peter **Taylor**, Zachariah **Dozier**, Boudy **Estill**, Samuel **Estill**, Joseph **Scott**, William **Dryden**, Aron **King**, Ambrose **Ross** were sworn a Grandjury for this County have receivd their charges retired to Consider of the presentments.

The Grandjury returned and made the following presentments.

Adam **Stearns** for retailing liquor without licence also the surveyor of the road from Paint Lick to the County line leading to the Crab Orchard.

Also the surveyor of the road from Robert **Henderson's** to the County line leading to Danville. Also the surveyor of the roads from William **Hancocks** to Boonsborough.

Present John **Miller** gent.

Thomas **Lewis** vs *Zachariah* **Dozier** office judgment set aside James Ingoe **Dozier** Special Baile non asst jd.

Robert **Hill** vs *Michael* **Woods** dismissed.

Same vs Same same order

Benjamin **Brown** vs *Baptist* **Clark**. Aron **King** Special Bail.

A deed from Higgason **Grubbs** to Edward **Turner** was acknowledged by Lucy **Grubbs** his wife she being first privately examined and Ordered to be recorded.

Order that William **Calk** and Aaron **Lewis** do examine into the capassity of Samuel **Davis** and George **Barnett** as deputy surveyors for this County and report the same.

A deed from Joseph and Andrew **Kennedy** to Boudy **Estill** was acknowledged and order to be recorded.

Ordered that Richard **Runnals** be appointed surveyor of the road in room of John **Doty**.

Ordered that a dedimiss issue to take the deposition of Richard **Eastin** and Andrew **Heath** as witnesses in the suit **Lewis** vs. *Zachariah* **Dozier**.

Ordered that John **Matthews** be appointed surveyor of the road leading from the mouth of Sugar Creek to intersect the Danville road near **Banks** in the room of John **Clark**. And that Moses **Dooley**, gent. be appointed to lott of the tithes to work on the same.

Ordered that Jesse **Hodges** be appointed Constable for this County.

Ordered that Nicholas **Hawkins** be appointed Constable for this County.

Ordered that John **Mounce** be appointed Constable in this County.

Ordered that Michael **Farris** be appointed Constable in this County.

Ordered that Aaron **Lewis** and John **Miller**, gent. be appointed to examine the surveyors and Clerk's offices of this County and make report in what manner they are kept.

Samuel **Davis** and George **Barnett** nominated by James **French** produced a certificate from the Examiners that they are capable and are appointed Deputy Surveyors in this County and took the oaths prescribed by Law.

Ordered that the Court be adjourned till Court in Course.

George **Adams**

At a Court held for Madison County on Tuesday the 25th of December 1787. Present George **Adams**, John **Snoddy**, David **Gass**, John **Boyle**, James **Barnet**, Archibald **Woods**, gent. Present John **Miller** gent.

Bennett **Pemberton**, gent. took the oath of fidelity and of Justice of the Peace and of Oyer and Terminer whereupon he is appointed to the said office. Present Bennett **Pemberton**.

A state of the County Levy for the year 1787. Tobc
To the Clerk for expens from August
   1786 till Aug 1787 1500
To the Sheriff for same 1500
To Thomas **Crews** for building a prison £ 45 7199
To Hugh **Campbell** for building temporary
   Courthouse £ 5-10 880
To Sheriff for tending on two examining Courts one
   on David **Hogen** and James **McManus** 400
To the Clerk for attending the same 400
To Thos **Hall** as one years sallery as D.S. Atty 1500
To Clerk for transmitting public claims 200
To Sheriffs Commissioners on collecting 1207
To a deposition .... <u>5342</u>
By 629 tithes at 32 pounds tobacco per Tithe 20128

   A deed from Higgerson **Grubbs** to Edward **Turner** was further proved by the oaths of Phillip **Turner** and John **Turner** and is ordered to be certified.

   Ordered that Andrew **Kennedy** be recommended to his Excellency the Govenor as a proper person to command as a Captain in Militia in this County.

   Ordered that Robert **Branks** be recommended to his Excellency the Governor as a proper person to command as a Lieutinant in the Militia of this County.

Ordered that Edward **Stephenson** be recommended to his Excellency the Govenor as a proper person to command as Ensign in the Militia in this County.

Order that Court adjourn till Court in Course.

George Adams

At a Court held for Madison County on Tuesday the 26th day of February 1788.

Present James **Barnett**, John **Boyles**, Archibald **Woods**, Moses **Dooley** and Bennett **Pemberton**, gent. Present Robert **Roads**.

Hannah **McNeely** orphan of James **McNeely**, deceased came into Court and made choice of Michael **McNeely** as her guardian who executed bond with Thomas **Kennedy** his security according to law.

Andrew **Kennedy** one of the Commissioners for Madison County come into Court and resigned his appointment to the said office.

Andrew **Kennedy** come into Court and made oath that he served twelve days as Commissioner in this County.

George **Adams**, gent. produced a Commission from the Governor of Virginia appointing him Sheriff for the County of Madison which being read he took the oath of fidelity to the Commonwealth and the oath of office and executed bond with James **Barnett**, Michael **McNeely**, Bennett **Pemberton** his securities conditioned as the law directs.

Ordered that Robert **Roads** be appointed Commissioner in the stead of Andrew **Kennedy** who hath resigned.

A power of Attorney from Edward **Praytor** to John **Praytor** was acknowledged and Ordered recorded.

Ordered that Cornelius **Daugherty** be summoned to shew cause why his daughter Isabel **Daugherty** should not be taken from under his direction for his ill treatment to her returnable to April Court next.

A report of a road from Madison Courthouse to **Estill's** Station Returned and Established and ordered that summons Issue to those persons whom the said road shall go through their lands.

Present--John **Snoddy**, Joseph **Kennedy** and John **Miller**, gent.

A power of attorney from Len Henly **Bullock** to Sherwood **Harris** was proved by oaths of Charles **Searcy** and is ordered to be recorded.

Ordered that William **Moore**, James **Adams**, John **Manire**, Uriah **Edwards**, David **Crews**, William **Jones**, John **Goggin**, Samuel **Estill** and Thomas **Shelton** be appointed Commissioner to act under the act directing the mode of proceeding of certain executions.

Robert **Rayburn** *assee* vs. *Hugh* **Ross** judgement of note for £ 1-16 *and costs.*

A deed from Higgarson **Grubbs** to William **Williams** was acknowledged and ordered to be recorded.

Thomas **Boyer** vs. *Joseph* **Scott** judgement for £ 4-14-4 *and costs.*

A deed from Higgerson **Grubbs** to Isaac **Williams** was acknowledged and ordered to be recorded.

Harris **Massie** assee vs. *Azariah* **Martines** judgment for £ 3-4 *and costs.*

A deed from Higgerson **Grubbs** to William **Pollard** was acknowledged and order to be recorded.

Ordered that the Court be adjourned till tomorrow 10 o'clock.

John Snoddy

At a Court held for Madison County on Wednesday 27th of February 1788.

Present John **Snoddy**, James **Barnett**, Archibald **Woods** and John **Miller**, gent.

Ordered that Samuel **Estill** make the necessary repairs to the Temporary Courthouse and that the expenses thereof be paid out the Depositum non loud agreeable to the direction of James **Barnett**, gent.

On motion of George **Adams**, Sheriff, John **Adams** is appointed Deputy Sheriff for the County of Madison and he took the oaths prescribed by Law.

Ordered that it is the oppinion of this Court that the goal is built agreeable to the dimentions specified in bond after the said *Thomas* **Crews** makes the following Repairs towit--the chimney to be raised six inches higher than the House and well plastered with lime mortor the floor cleand and the earth removed from the door as soon as the weather admit of-

Present Joseph **Kennedy**, gent.

Absent Archibald **Woods**, gent.

George **Adams**, Sheriff came into Court and enters his objection as to the sufficiency of the Goal.

Present Archibald **Woods**, gent.

Ordered that a Courthouse be built agreeable to a plan lodged in the office.

Ordered that David **Gass**, Joseph **Kennedy** and John **Miller**, gent. be appointed to let the building of a Courthouse for this County and that a copy of the plan lodge in the office be sent to Commissioners appointed.

Ordered that Aaron **Lewis** and Robert **Roads**, gent. be appointed to apportion tithes to work on road. William **Orear**, James **Hendricks**, David **Crews**, Robert **Roads** and George **Boon**.

Ordered that Court adjourn til Court in Course.

John **Snoddy**

At a Court of Quarter Session held at Madison Courthouse on Tuesday the 25th of March 1788.

Present John **Snoddy**, James **Barnett**, John **Boyle**, Joseph **Kennedy**, Archibald **Woods**, Robert **Roads**, Bennett **Pemberton**.

Michael **McNeely**, foreman; John **Kennedy**, Andrew **Kennedy**, Ambrose Ross, Joseph **Scott**, William **Handcock**, Peter **Owsley**, John **Maxwell**, David **Maxwell**, Richard **Walker**, Robert **Henderson**, Humphrey **Best**, James **Crawford**, Henry **Owley**, Cornelius **Daugherty**, John **Anderson** were sworn a Grand Jury for this County discharged til tomorrow 10 o'clock.

Present David **Gass** and Aaron **Lewis**, gent.

Ordered that the Court adjourn till Tomorrow 10 o'clock.

John **Snoddy**

At a Court continued Wednesday 26th 1788.

Present John **Snoddy**, David **Gass**, James **Barnett**, Archibald **Woods**, Joseph **Kennedy** and Bennett **Pemberton**, gent.

Andrew **Kennedy**, gent produced a Commission from his Excellency the Governor appointing him Captain in the Militia of this County and he took the Oath prescribed by Law.

On motion of George **Adams**, gent. Andrew **Miller** is appointed his Deputy and that he took the oath prescribd by Law.

Ordered that Mathw **Adams** be recommended to his Excellency the Governer as a proper person to be commissioned as Lieutenant in the Militia in this County and Andrew **Miller** as Ensign.

Present John **Boyles**, gent.

Ordered that Samuel **Estill** be permitted to build on the lands condemned for public buildings for this County.

Ordered that Richard **Walker** and Robert **Kincaid** be summons to appear at the next Court to shew cause why they did not attend as Grand Jurors.

Present John **Miller** and Aaron **Lewis**.

The persons appointed to settle the account of James **Robinson** [*Robertson*] as administrator to the Estate of James **McNeely**, deceased produced the account and the matter is continued untill next Court and it is ordered that the said **Robinson** [*Robertson*] be notified of the same.

Thomas **Brown** vs. Hugh **Ross** judgment on Replevy Bond. £ 4-6-11 and interest from 20 November 1787 and costs.

Order that Aaron **King** be summons to appear at the next Court to answer how much of the Estate of Charles **Chafrey**, deceased he has in his hands.

Ordered that George **Adams**, gent. do pay to the person holding of a bond Given for the Building of the Public Goal the amount of the money now in his hands collected on the County Levey and that he have Credit on the bond for the amount so paid and take a receipt for the same.

Ordered that Hugh and John **Campbell** do apply to Joseph **Kennedy** former Shrff for £ 5-10 for Building a Temporary Courthouse.

Ordered that James **Robertson** administrator of James **McNeely** deceased do Deliver unto George **Adams** and Michael **McNeely** the bonds and other papers necessary and for the collection for the money due to the said estate.

Absent Joseph **Kennedy**, John **Miller** and David **Gass**, gent.

Ordered that the Ferry on the south side of the river at Boonsborough to the opposite shore be vested in Caleb **Callaway**, Fanny **Holder**, Lydia **Irvine**, Doshia **Callaway**, Cuzza **French**, Richard **Callaway** and John **Callaway** to them their heirs or assigns forever to hold as Tenants in Common and not as Joint Tenants.

Ordered that rates of crossing at the above ferry be as follows: three pense for a man three pence for a horse and for other things in proportion as the Law directs.

Madison County, Kentucky Court Order Book A 33

John **Mitchell** vs *Green* **Clay** comn writ inquiry set aside Samuel **Estill** Special Bail plead non assmt.

Ordered that Samuel **Estill** be appointed guardian for Benjamine **Estill**, Wallace **Estill**, James **Estill**, Jonathan **Estill** and Sarrah **Estill** orphans of James **Estill** deceased. Whereupon he Entered into bond conditioned as the Law directs. *Securities are Archibald* **Woods**, *James* **Black** *and Green* **Clay**.

Order that Thomas **Shelton**, James **French** and William **Irvine** be appointed to settle with Nicholas and Rachel **Proctor** as administrator to the estate of James **Estill** deceased and that they make a return to the next Court.

Ordered that the first Plan filed in the Clerk's Office for building a Courthouse for this County be set aside and that it be Built agreeable to a plan now filed in the office.

Ordered that Green **Clay** be recommended to his Excellency the Governor as a proper person to be appointed as Captain of the Militia *Cavalry* in this County and Thomas **Gass** as Lieutenant and John **Gass** as Cornet.

John **Gass** producd a Commission from his Excellency the Governor appointing him Cornet in the Militia Cavalry for this County whereupon he took the oath prescribd by Law.

Ordered that Samuel **Estill** be allowed nine shillings for work done to the temporary Courthouse.

Ordered that Matthew **Walton**, James **French** and William **Irvine** Enter into Bond with sufficient security at the next Court for keeping the Ferry at Boonsborough in such repair as the Law requires.

Ordered that John **Snoddy**, David **Gass** and James **Barnett**, gent. be appointed to settle with Joseph **Kennedy**, late Sheriff, and make a report to next Court.

Ordered that Court adjourn till Court in Course.
                    John **Snoddy**

At a Court held for the County of Madison at the Courthouse on Tuesday the 22nd day of April 1788.

Present John **Snoddy**, David **Gass**, James **Barnett**, John **Boyles**, Archibald **Woods**, Joseph **Kennedy**, Robert **Roads**, Bennett **Pemberton**, gent.

A deed from William **Robertson** *and Sarah his wife* to Nicholas **Hawkins** was acknowledged and ordered to be recorded. Fem relinquished.

Ordered that Richard **Walker** and John **Smith** be summoned to appear at next Court to show cause why they should not be fined and *trible taxed* for refusing to give in their Lists on Oath. Also Samuel **Harris**, Thomas **Harris**, Jeremiah **McCarty** and George **Yocum** for not appearing to give in their list when required by the Commissioners.

Ordered that Samuel **Woods** be appointed surveyor of the road leading from Paint Lick to the Crab Orchard on room of Samuel **Gordon** and that the said **Gorden** be exempted from personal service on the highways.

Ordered that the Court Adjourn till tomorrow 10 o'clock.

John **Snoddy**

At a Court held and continued on Wednesday 23rd April 1788.

Present John **Snoddy**, David **Gass**, John **Boyles**, Archibald **Woods**, Bennett **Pemberton** and Moses **Dooley**, gent.

On motion of George **Adams**, sheriff, William **Orear** is appointed his Deputy whereupon he took the Oaths prescribed by Law.

John **Maniere** produced a Nomination from James **French** as one of his Deputies Whereupon William **Calk** and John **Adams** is appointed to examine into his Capacity as Deputy Surveyor and make report thereof to this Court.

A deed from James **Knox** attorney in fact for Alexander **Sinclair** to John **Biswell** is acknowledged and ordered to be recorded.

A deed from James **Knox** attorney in fact for Alex **Sinclair** to Rabbi **Brown** was acknowledged and ordered to be recorded.

Ordered that John **Mounce**, *Senior* and John **Mounce**, *Junior* be exempted from paying County and Parish levy.

Ordered that it be certified to Edmund **Randolph**, Esqr. Governor of Virginia that George **Adams**, gent. Sheriff of the County of Madison has been Duly Call upon to give Security for the collection of the Tax arising under the present revenue law and that he has refused to give security for the collection of the same.

Absent John **Snoddy**, gent.

Ordered that the account of James **Robinson** [*Robertson*] administrator on the Estate of James **McNeely** deceased be set aside and that John **Boyle**,

Madison County, Kentucky Court Order Book A   35

James **Barnett**, Alexander **Reed** and Alexander **Denny** do again examine and settle the Accounts of the said James **Robinson** [*Robertson*] administrator as aforesaid and make report to next June Court.
    Present John **Snoddy**.
    Nathaniel **Logan** asee vs Bartholomew **Fenton** continued.
    A deed from Green **Clay** to Edward **Williams** was acknowledged and ordered recorded.
    James A. **Sturgis** vs. Azariah **Martin** judgment for £ 13-17 and costs.
    Ordered that Court adjourn till Court in Course.
                    John **Snoddy**

At a Court called and held at Madison Courthouse on Wednesday 23rd April 1788 for the examination of Isaac **Burton** and Sarah his wife charged with the robbing James **Durham** of sundrie goods before the worshipful Court of John **Snoddy**, David **Gass**, James **Barnett**, John **Boyles**, Archibald **Woods**, Bennett **Pemberton** and John **Miller**, gent.
    Upon sundry witnesses being examined and the prisoners heard in their defense. It is the opinion of this Court that they be acquitted and discharge from the aforesaid charge. The Court then dissolved.
                    John **Snoddy**

At a Court of Quarter Session held for Madison County at the Courthouse on Tuesday the 27th day of May 1788.
    Present John **Snoddy**, John **Boyles**, Archibald **Woods**, James **Kennedy**, Robert **Roads** and Bennett **Pemberton**, gent.

    Ordered that James **Tilly** and James **Tilly**, Junr. be exempted from paying the County Levey.
    Ordered that Thomas **Farris** be exempted from paying County levy.
    Present James **Barnett**.
    A power of attorney from Charles **Kavanaugh** to William **Kavanaugh** was acknowledged and Ordered recorded.
    James **Brown**, Esqr. produced a licence to practice as an Attorney at Law whereupon he took the oaths prescribed by Law.
    Ordered that Jeremiah **McCarty** and Edward **Moss** be exempt from paying County levy for the year 1787.

Ordered that John **Clark** and James **Clark** be Exempt from paying County Levy.

Michael **McNeely**, foreman; Stephen **Hancock**, William **Turpen**, John **Orchard**, Edward **Turner**, Robert **Moore**, William **Handcock**, Zach **Dozier**, Peter **Taylor**, Henry **Owley**, Richard **Walker**, Thomas **Kennedy**, Peter **Owley**, Humphrey **Best**, John **Anderson**, John **Maxwell**, Samuel **Gordon**, Robert **Henderson** and Boud **Estill** was sworn a Grand Jury having received there Charges retired to Consider of there presentments.

A deed from Hugh **Campbell** and ux to Robert **Kilpatrick** was acknowledged and Ordered recorded. Feme relinquished.

Ordered that Thomas **Harris** be fined ten shillings for drunkness and missbehaviour and insulting the Court.

William **Bowman** who was brought in to Court to answer a complaint of misbehavior whereupon he entered into recognizance with Joseph **Kennedy** his security the said **Bowman** in the sum of forty pounds and the said **Kennedy** in the sum of twenty that is if the said **Bowman** shall be of good behavior towards all the Commonwealths Lieje people for one year.

Ordered that Moses **Dooley** and James **Finney** be recommended to his Excellency as proper persons to be commissioned as Ensigns in the Militia in this County.

Ordered that John **Wilson** be recommended to his Excellency as a proper person to be commissioned as Captain, Isaac **Mize** as Lieutenant and Edward **Parker** as Ensign in Militia in this County.

Ordered that Thomas **Warren** be appointed surveyor of the road from **Estills** Station to the Courthouse and that Archibald **Woods**, gent. is appointed to lott the tiths to work on the same.

Ordered that Thomas **Stevens** be appointed surveyor of the road in the place of William **Orear**.

The Grand Jury Returned and made the following presentment Thomson **Harris** for profane swearing also for getting drunk and roiting.

Commonwealth vs Samuel **Rice**. A True Bill.

William **Sprowl** vs Joseph **Scott**. Joseph **Kennedy** Special Bail.

Commonwealth vs Joseph **Scott** Discontinued.

Same vs Haile **Talbot** Discontinued.

Same vs Peter **Taylor** judgment according to Law. *4 shillings each for profane swearing and getting drunk.*

Same vs Same judgment for drunkeness.
Same vs William **Orear** Discontinued.
Same vs Edmund **Terrel** Discontinued.
Same vs Samuel **Gordon** Discontinued.
Same vs James **Hendrick** discontinued.
William **Robertson** vs Edward **Moss**. Boud **Estill** Special Bail.
William **Wycoff** vs John **Mounce** judgment for four pounds four shillings eleven pence.
Nathaniel **Logan** vs Bartholomew **Fenton** Dismissed.
Cornelius **Daugherty** vs Andrew **Woods** dismissed.
John **McClure** vs James **Mason** judgment for one pound eight shillings and six pence.
George **Gray** vs *Weldon* **South**. John **South** Special Bail.
Christopher **Chinn's** Executors vs William **Moore** continued for defendant.
William **Stafford** vs Hugh **Ross** judgment for 50/ and costs. £ *2-10*.
Edward **Williams** vs Thomas **Gass** continued.
William **Young** vs Edward **Shackelford** judgment £ *1-10 and costs*.
Thomas **Perkins** administrators vs William **Dryden** *judgment granted Plaintiff* two pounds and three shillings.
James **Robertson** vs Anthony **Rogers** judgment according to note *and costs*.
Mary **Crawford** vs William **Poe** judgment for £ *1-15 and costs*.
Ordered that Thomson **Harris** be committed to jail for misbehavior and contempt to this Court.
On the motion of John **Holly** a licence is granted him to retail all kind of goods, wares and Merchandise in the Town of Boonsborough.
Ordered that the Court be adjourned untill Court in Course.

John **Snoddy**

At a Court held for Madison at Courthouse on Tuesday 24th day June 1788.
Present John **Snoddy**, David **Gass**, Archibald **Woods** and Bennett **Pemberton**, gent.

Richard **Masterson** vs *Hugh* **Ross** judgment on replevy bond. £ *3-7-10 and costs*.

Ordered that certificate be granted Charles **Kavanaugh**, Senr. that satisfactory prove was made to this Court that he is eldest son to Philemon **Kavanaugh**, Deceased formerly of Culpeper Co.

A deed from Green **Clay** to **John Davis** was proved by the oaths Dukrey **Barkshire**, Samuel **Davis** and Edward **Durbin** and Ordered recorded.

A deed from Green **Clay** to James **Harris** was proved by the oaths of Edward **Durbin**, Joseph **Durbin** and Richard **Fowler** and Ordered recorded.

Present James **Barnett** and Joseph **Kennedy**, gent.

Ordered that John **Carpenter** and Archibald **Woods** be permitted to build a mill across Otter Creek from opposite where the said **Carpenter** now lives to the other shore.

Christopher **Harris** his Earmark a crop slit and under keel in the right ear and slit and under keel in the left is Ordered recorded.

Present Aron **Lewis**, gent.

Ordered that the surveyor of this County do lay off two acres land for the use of the public buildings in this County. Agreable to the courses and bounds already prescribed to him by the Court and that he drive up stakes at each corner.

Ordered that the Surveyor of this County do lay of the bounds as followeth beginning at where the old road crosses the creek therewith the meanders of the said creek and road so far as two other lines will include the Quantity of ten acres to include the two acres layed of for the public buildings and make report to the Court.

Ordered that Philip **Hogen** be exempted from paying County and Parish levey.

Ordered that John **Holly** and Charles **Debrial** be recommended as proper persons to be added to the Commission of the peace in this County.

Ordered that a Dedimus Issue for taking the Deposition of Nicholas **Hawkins** in the suit *William* **Robertson** vs *Edward* **Moss** Debeneesse.

Absent James **Barnett** and Joseph **Kennedy**, gent.

Ordered that John **Holley**, Jacob **Miller**, Peter **Woods** and Archibald **Woods** or any three of them do view the nearest and best way for a road from Boonsborough to Archibald **Woods** and make report.

Ordered that John **Woodroff** be appointed surveyor of the road from his house to the three mile tree between there and Boonsborough and that Aron **Lewis**, gent. be appointed to lott of the tith to work on the same.

Ordered that David **Crews** extend his Road from the mouth of Jacks Creek to John **Colliers**.

Ordered that William **Williams**, William **Jones**, Robert **Rodes** and John **Wilson** be appointed to view the nearest and best way for a road from John **Collier's** to intersect the road from the mouth of Tates Creek to the Courthouse and make report.

Ordered that John **Collier** be summoned to appear at the next Court to say if he will undertake the building of the public whearhouse establishd by Law at his house.

Present Joseph **Kennedy**, gent.

Ordered that the Court adjourned untill Court in Course.

John Snoddy

At a Court held at Madison Courthouse on Tuesday 22nd day of July 1788.

Present John **Snoddy**, James **Barnett**, Archibald **Woods**, Robert **Rodes**, Bennett **Pemberton** and Moses **Dooly**, gent.

A deed from George **Adams** to James **Adams** was acknowledged and Ordered recorded.

Commonwealth vs James **Martin** Discontinued with costs.

Moses **Dooley** produced a Commission from his Excellency appointing him Ensign in the Militia in this County whereupon he took the oaths prescribed by Law.

Ordered that Charles **Kavanaugh**, Senr. be exempted from personal service on all public roads.

Ordered that Frances **Taylor** be exempted from paying County levey.

A report of a road from *John* **Colliers** wherehouse to intersect the road from the mouth of Tates Creek is established and Ordered recorded. And John **Wilson** is appointed surveyor of the said road and Robert **Roades**, gent. is appointed to lott of the tithes to work on the same.

John **Wilson** produced a commission from his Excellency appointing him Captain in the Militia in this County whereupon he took the oath prescribed by law.

A Report of a Road from Boonsborough to Archibald **Woods** was returned and establish and Ordered recorded. Ordered that Francis **Holley** be appointed surveyor of the said road from Boonsborough to Carr **Smith** and

Peter **Woods** from thence to Archibald **Woods** and Archibald **Woods**, gent. is appointed to lott of the tithes to work on the said roads.

Present David **Gass**.

The surveyor of this County returned a list of surveys recorded in his office since the 24th day of July 1787 which is Ordered recorded.

Ordered that Stephen **Hancock** be appointed surveyor of the *road from Archibald* **Woods** *to Taylor Fork* in the room of Peter **Woods**.

Ordered that Robert **Rodes** be Exempt from paying County levy for his negroe **Jane** [*Fanny*].

Ordered that Joseph **Ray** be permitted to build a mill on Back Creek from his land on one side to his on the other.

The surveyor of this County according to ordered returned a survey of the two acres of land layd off for use of the Public Building and ten acres for the prison rules which is Ordered recorded.

Ordered that David **Coomley** be appointed surveyor of the Road from the *Lincoln* County line to Back Creek and Benett **Pemberton** to lott of the tithes or to divide them between him and Edmund **Terrel**.

Ordered that Thomas **Baker** be appointed surveyor of the road in the room of Hail **Talbot**.

Ordered that a Ferry be Established in the name of William **Turpen** across the Kentucky River to the oposit shore from nearly opposit where the said **Turpen** now lives.

Ordered that the rate for crossing at the Ferry be as followeth towit. Three pense for man and the same for a horse and so in proportion as the Laws directs for other things.

Ordered that John **Snoddy** and David **Gass**, gent. be recommend as proper persons to be Commissioned as Sheriff in this County.

Ordered that Court do adjourned until Court in Course.

John **Snoddy**

At a Court of Quarter Session held a Madison Courthouse on Tuesday 26th day August 1788.

Present John **Snoddy**, David **Gass**, Archibald **Woods**, Robert **Roads**, Bennett **Pemberton** and John **Miller**, gent.

A deed from James **Crawford** and *Rebeckah his wife* to David **Rice** was acknowledged and Ordered recorded. Feme relinquished.

Present Aaron **Lewis**, gent.

Thomas **Kennedy**, foreman; Samuel **Jameson**, Edward **Turner**, Samuel **Freeman**, Boud **Estill**, Timothy **Logan**, William **Hancock**, Humphrey **Best**, John **Kincaid**, Robert **Moore**, James **Crawford**, Ambrose **Ross**, Samuel **Gordon**, Michael **McNeely**, Peter **Wooly**, Robert **Henderson** and John **Maxwell** received their Charge returned to consider of their presentments.

William **Murray**, Esqr. produced a licence to practice as an attorney at Law and thereupon took the oaths required by Law.

Ordered that Christopher **Harris** be Exempted from paying a County levy for one black tithe which he is charged with more than he has.

Ordered that John **Prater** be recommended to his Excellency as a proper person to be commissioned as a Ensign in this County.

The Grand Jury returned and presented John **Martin** for profane swearing.

Michael **McNeely** came into Court and made oath that he had served fifteen days as a Commissioner.

Gorden and **Coburn** vs Jonathan **Longstreeth**. John **Bruce** Special Bail judgment confessed according to Specialty. Plaintiff by his attorney consented to stay of Execution for six months.

John **Courbourn** vs Same. John **Bruce** Special Bail Judgment confessed and to sheriff and to stay Execution six months.

Christopher **Greenup**, Esqr. produced licence to practice as an attorney at Law whereas he took the oaths prescribed by Law.

Robert **Brooks** vs John **Anderson** Continued at the defendant costs.
John **Cline** vs John **McMahan** continued.
James **McMahan** [*McManus*] vs John **Owins** Dissmissed.
Richard **Runnalds** vs Baptis **Clark** Dismissed.
Christopher **Wooley** [*Owley*] vs John **McMahan** Dismissed.
Baptist **Clark** vs Hugh **Ross** Continued
Chins Executors vs William **Moor** Continued
Edward **Williams** vs Thomas **Guist** judgment for £ 3-10-0.
Robert **Terrel** vs William **Moore** judgment £ 3-16-0.
William **McClure** vs John **Collier** Discontinued.
Thomas **Kennedy** vs Benjamin **Proctor** Continued.

A deed from John **Tanner** and *Rachel his wife* to David **Crews** was acknowledged and Ordered recorded. Feme Relinquished.

A deed from William **Hoy** to David **Crews** was acknowledged and Ordered recorded.

John **Lewis** vs *Zachariah* **Dozier** judgment confessed for costs.

Same vs Same. Same order.

A deed from John **Tanner** and *Rachel his wife* to Archibald **Woods** was Acknowledged and Ordered recorded. Feme relinquished.

A deed from John **Tanner** and *Rachel his wife* to Absolem **Crook** was acknowledged and Ordered recorded. Feme relinquished.

Aaron **King** who was summoned and sworn *to declare what property he hath in his hands belonging* to Charles **Chalfrey**, deceased declares he has £ 1-10 which is condemned in his hands.

Robert **Henry** vs Jeremiah **Parker** judgment £ 3 and costs.

A deed from William **Hoy** to Joshua **McQueen** was acknowledged and Ordered recorded.

A deed from John **Tanner** and *Rachel his wife* to William **Hoy** acknowledged and Ordered recorded. Femme Relinquished.

A deed from William **Hoy** to Dotson **Thorp** was acknowledged and Ordered recorded.

A deed from John **Tanner** and *Rachel his wife* to Charles **Ballou** was acknowledged and Ordered recorded. Femme Relinquished.

Edward **Williams** to pay Dennis **Bergen** for 2 days vs *Thomas* **Gass**.

Same to pay Joseph **Butcher** 4 days Ditto.

Same to pay William **Williams** 2 days Ditto.

Thomas **Gass** to pay Jesse **Noland** for 2 days against *Edward* **Williams**.

Robert **Henry** to pay Bartholomew **Fenton** for today vs **Parker**.

James **Hinds** vs *Joseph* **Merrit**. Higgason **Grubbs** Special Bail.

Ordered that Bartholomew **Fenton** be appointed Constable in this County.

Thomas **Gass** to pay John **Tanner** for 9 days and riding 39[*78*] miles against **Williams**.

Ordered that the Court be adjourned until tomorrow ten o'clock.

John **Snoddy**

Madison County, Kentucky Court Order Book A 43

At a Court continued and held at Madison Courthouse on Wednesday the 27th August 1788.

Present Jospeh **Kennedy**, John **Snoddy**, David **Gass**, Aaron **Lewis**, Moses **Dooley** and John **Miller**, gent.

William **Robertson** vs Edward **Moss** Jury sworn to try the Issue towit. Edward **Turner**, Hugh **Campbell**, David **Lynch**, Samuel **Estil**, William **Turpin**, James **Berry**, Baptist **Clark**, Alex **Canny**, Peter **Taylor**, John **Mitchell**, William **Kerly** and William **Calk** returned. The plaintiff not appearing a non suit.

John **Kincaid** vs Thomas **Kennedy** judgment £ 3-12-6 and costs.

Zachariah **Dozier** v *Peter* **Evans** Continued.

John **Kincaid** v *Azariah* **Martin** Dismissed.

Patrick **Lockhart** & Co v *Thomas* **Welch** Continued and on the Motion and oath of the Defendant a Dedimus is granted to *take the deposition of* John **Thompson**, Samuel **Amocks** and Matthew **Amocks**.

Edward **Moss** to pay John **Chiles** for 2 days and 25 Miles against **Robertson** [*William Roberts*].

Same to pay Thomas **Campbell** 1 day against Ditto.

Same to pay James **Howard** 2 days against Ditto.

Same to pay Joseph **Butcher** for 2 days <u>not taxed</u>.

Same to pay William **Butcher** for 2 days against Ditto.

Robertson to pay Robert **Kirkpatrick** 2 days vs *Edward* **Moss**.

Same to pay William **Briscoe** 2 days *against Edward Moss.*

Moses **Hall** v *Joseph* **Kennedy** judgment £ 1-16 and costs.

Moses **Hall** to pay Edward **Hall** 2 days traveling 30 miles vs *Joseph* **Kennedy**.

Henry **French** vs *Hugh* **Ross** judgment and Interest *from the 25th November 1787* and note and Costs. *£ 3-6-6.*

Same vs *James* **Crawford** same order. *£ 4 and interest from the 19th September 1787 and costs.*

James **Smith** vs *Aquilla* **White** Continued.

Alexander **Orr** v. *Ralph* **Morgan** Jury sworn to inquire of damages towit. John **South**, Senr. Flanders **Callaway**, Samuel **South**, Valentine **Stone**, John **Holly**, Thomas **Warren**, Jacob **Starns**, David **Crews**, William **Briscoe**,

Humphry **Best**, Robert **Deane** and Alex **Reid** returned verdict for Plaintiff £ 9-18-6 debt £ 15-2 3/4 damages and judgment.

An Estate account of James **McNealys** was returned into Court by the persons who settled the same and ordered to be recorded.

Humphrey **Best** v *Thomas* **Kennedy** Continued.

Robert **Deane** v *Robert* **Branks** dismissed at plaintiff's costs.

Samuel **Coughran** v **Branks** *and Azariah* **Martin** Jury Sworn to Inquire of damages towit. Hugh **Campbell**, James **Berry**, Nicholas **Proctor**, John **Mitchel**, Benjamin **Cooper**, William **Robertson**, David **Lynch**, Peter **Taylor**, William **Kerley**, Peter **Hacket**, William **Anderson** and John **Black** returned verdict for plaintiff. £ 16-5 damages and costs.

On motion of Thomas **Baker** his Earmark a Crop in the right Ear and a half crop in the left and Ordered recorded.

Ordered that it be Certified to the Register of the Land office that Benjamin **Estill** is the Eldest Son of James **Estill**, deceased.

Walker **Daniels** administrators vs *William* **Calk** Continued.

William **Holland** v *Robert* **Burton** Continued.

William **Sprowl** vs *Joseph* **Scott** writ of Inquiry set aside and cod perf'd j.d. *Defendant says that he had well and truly kept and performed the conditions in the writing mentioned.*

George **Gray** vs *Weldon* **South** continued.

John **Martin** vs *James* **French** Continued.

James **Robertson** vs *Hugh* **McCormack**, *Thomas* **Daniel** *and Joseph* **Scott.** Dismissed.

Benjamin **Brown** vs *Baptist* **Clark** Continued at plaintiff's costs.

John **Adams** vs *Charles* **Chalfrey** administrator Continued.

William **Thomas** v *Uriah* **Edwards** Continued.

Ordered that William **Finney** be appointed surveyor of the Road from the north east side of paint Lick to intersect the road below Joseph **Ray** and Joseph **Kennedy** gent to lott of the tithes to work on same.

William **Robertson** to pay Alexander **Reed** 2 day vs *Edward* **Moss**.

Ordered that the Court be adjourned until Court in Course.

John **Snoddy**

At a Court held at Madison Courthouse on Tuesday the 23rd of September 1788.

Madison County, Kentucky Court Order Book A   45

Present John **Snoddy**, David **Gass**, Joseph **Kennedy**, Aaron **Lewis**, Benett **Pemberton** and John **Miller**, gent.

The Reverend Thomas **Williamson** produced a certificate of his being in Regular Communion with the methodist Church whereupon a licence to Celebrate the Right of Marriage.

A deed from Green **Clay** to Benjamin **Oakley** was provd by the oath of John **Wilson**, Joel **Hill**, William **Oakley** and is Ordered recorded.

A deed from Green **Clay** to John **Wilson** was proved by the oath of Benjamin **Oakley**, William **Oakley** and Joel **Hill** and is Ordered recorded.

A deed from G **Clay** to Joel **Hill** was proved by the oath of Benjamin **Oakley**, William **Oakley** and John **Wilson** was Ordered recorded.

Daniel **Boone** who was nominated by James **French** as one of his deputy whereupon Aron **Lewis** and William **Calk** is appointed to examine him as a surveyor and make report to the Court.

A power of attorney from Elizabeth **Callaway** to James **French** was proved by the oath of Richard **Callaway** and Daniel **Baty** and Ordered recorded.

A deed from William **Irvine** attorney in fact for Jesse **Cartright** to Humphrey **Arnold** was acknowledged and Ordered recorded.

Samuel **Rice** against of the Commonwealth a dedimis is awarded him to take the deposition of James **Tilley**, Patsey **Tilley** and Jane **Tilley** De be niesse.

Ordered that John **Colier** be appointed to build a public wherehouse at the place appointed by Law on the said **Collier** land. The house to be about 24 feet by 18 and Aron **Lewis** and Robert **Rodes**, gent. is appointed as Commissioners to superintend the said buildings and to bond of the said **Collier** for the true performance of the same.

Aaron **Lewis** vs *James I.* **Dozier** a dedemus is Ordered to take the deposition of Samuel and Welden **South** do be neisse.

Ordered Aaron **Lewis** and Robert **Rodes**, gent do with the assistance of the surveyor lay of one acre of land at the most convenient place on the land of John **Collier** for the purpose of erecting of a public wherehouse on.

Order that James **French** surveyor of this County have leave of absence from this County untill the 25th day of December next and Aaron **Lewis**, gent.

is approved by this Court to superintend the business of his office in his absence.

Order that Boud **Estill** be appointed survey of the Road in the Room of Hugh **Campbell** and David **Gass**, gent. is appointed to lott of the tiths to work on the same.

Order that David **Crews**, John **South**, William **Jones** and John **Collier** be Recommended as proper persons to be Commissioned as inspectors for the wherehouses at John **Collier** and Boonsborough.

Order that John **Sapington** be recommended as a proper persons to be commissioned as a Captain in the Militia, Joseph **Logsdon** Lieutenant and Page **Portwood** as Ensign.

Ordered that John **Holly** be summoned to appear at the next Court to declare if he will undertake the building of the public wherehouse at Boonsborough.

John **Miller** made oath that he had served ten days as a Commissioner in this County and certificate is to Issue for the same.

Order that it be certified to the Register Land Office that Thomas **Kennedy** is the Elder brother of John **Kennedy**, deceased.

Order that the Court adjourned until Court in Course.

John **Snoddy**

At a Court *of Quarter Session* held at Madison Courthouse on Tuesday the 25th day of October 1788.

Present John **Snoddy**, David **Gass**, Joseph **Kennedy**, Archibald **Woods**, *Robert Rodes,* Bennett **Pemberton** and Moses **Dooley** gent.

A deed from Higgason **Grubbs** and *Lucy his wife* to William **Denham** was acknowledged and Ordered recorded. Feme relinquished.

A power of attorney from Jesse [*Jestinean*] **Cartright** to William **Irvine** was proved by the oaths of William **Adam** [*Mann*] and Ordered recorded.

Michael **McNeely***,* foreman; Andrew **Kennedy**, John **Kennedy**, James **Crawford**, Thymoly **Logan**, Robert **Henderson**, Humphrey **Best**, James **Adams**, Richard **Walker**, Cornelius **Daugherty**, Lofty **Pullin**, William **Robertson**, Josiah **Phelps**, John **Bruse**, Robert **Moore**, Higgason **Grubbs**, Zach **Dozier**, John **Anderson** and William **Miller** was sworn a Grand Jury for this County having received their charge retired to consider of their presentments.

A deed from George **Adams** to James **Mason** was acknowledged and Ordered recorded.

Ordered that it be insert that the Court has Leave from the person building the new Courthouse to set in the same until it is finished and also that the sheriff make sail of the Tempo Courthouse and give Credit *to the purchaser* untill June next.

Ordered that Alexander **McKay**, Christopher **Harris** and John **Manier** be appointed and authorized to Celebrate the Rights of Marriage whereupon the said **McKay** and **Manier** entered into bond Conditioned as the Law directs.

Ordered that Reubin **Searcy**, Esqr. be recommended to the Honorable the Judges of the Supreme Court for the District of Kentucky as a Person of Honesty, Probity and good demeanor in Order to obtain a licence to practice as an attorney in the County or other inferior Courts in the said District.

Order that Robert **Moore** be appointed surveyor of the Road in Room of Robert **Rodes**.

Ordered that Thomas **Crews** be summoned to appear at the next Court to show cause why he has not made the necessary repairs to the Jail in this County.

On the motion of Andrew **Woods** his Earmark the right cropped and a slit and a slit in the left is Ordered recorded.

The Grand Jury returned and made the following presentments.

William **Morrison,** James **Martin,** Hugh **Kilpatrick,** John **Pitman,** Joseph **Scott,** Joseph **Merit,** Thomas **Kennedy** and Jeremiah **Perry** and it is ordered the said persons be summoned to appear *at the next County Quarter Session.*

A Deed from Robert **Henderson** to Stephen **Merrit** was acknowledged and Returned with the Memorandum.

Ordered that Aaron **Lewis** and Robert **Rodes**, gent. be appointed to Lay off one acre of Land at Boonsborough for the purpose of Erecting a public whearhouse on.

On motion of Samuel **Rice** and on making the usual Oath a Dedimus issue to Daniel **James** for said **Rice** against the Commonwealth.

James **Smith** vs *Aquilla* **White** Continued.

Comwealth vs **Rice** Oyer.
Hump **Best** vs Thomas **Kennedy** Continued.
William **Holland** vs Robert **Benton** Continued.
John **Martin** assee vs *James* **French** Continued.
John **Mitchell** vs *Green* **Clay** Continued.
Commonwealth against Samuel **Rice**--*Indictment.*

Joseph **Moore** came into Court and produced a Receipt signed by Robert **Brownfield** for a note received of John **Moore** on John **Morgan** for thirteen pounds and also satisfactory proof was made that the said note was not delivered for any consideration but only to collect the Debt and Order to be certified.

Ordered that the Court be adjourned until Tomorrow morning 10 oclock.

John **Snoddy**

At a Court *of Quarter Session* continued and held at Madison Courthouse on Wednesday the 29th of October 1788.

Present John **Snoddy**, David **Gass**, John **Boyles**, Archibald **Woods**, Joseph **Kennedy** and Aaron **Lewis**, gent.

Walker **Daniels** administrators vs *William* **Calk** Judgment Confessed £ *10* with Interest from the first of April 1784[*last*].

William **Calk** one of George **Adams** Deputies came into Court and took the Oaths Prescribed by Law.

Present Robert **Rodes**, gent.

John **Gunnel** vs William **Hoy** judgment for debt and costs. *£ 4-13-9*

Baptist **Clark** vs Hugh **Ross** Continued.

John **Adams** vs *Chalfrys* administrator (*Michael McNeely*) Jury Sworn to Enquire of Damages towit. John **Kincaid**, John **Butler**, William **Chennault**, Nicholas **Proctor**, Lewis **Dewes**, Andrew **Kennedy**, James **Black**, Cornelius **Daugherty**, Thomas **Warren**, Edmund **Herring**, Jesse **Hodges**, James **Martin** returned a verdict for Plaintiff £ 10 damages and judgment.

Thomas **Kennedy** vs Benjamin **Proctor** Continued.

James **Martin** vs *John* **Kincaid** writ of Inquiry set aside and paiment paid. *The defendant says that he has well and timely kept and performed the several conditions in the writing mentioned.*

Madison County, Kentucky Court Order Book A 49

William **Sprowl** vs *Joseph* **Scott** Continued at Defendant Costs.
George **Grey** vs *Weldon* **South** *In Trespass* Continued.
Michael **McNeely** to pay William **Miller** 2 days attendance against *John* **Adams**.
Benjamin **Brown** vs *Baptist* **Clark** Continued.
William **Thomas** vs *Uriah* **Edwards** Jury sworn to inquire of Damages towit. Haile **Talbot**, John **Anderson**, Robert **Moore**, Page **Portwood**, John **Johnson**, Thomas **Butler**, Alexander **Eoff** [*Offe*], Thomas **Campbell**, David **Crews**, William **Robertson**, John **South** and Higgason **Grubbs** returned verdict for Plaintiff £ 22-6-4 Debt and Damages judgment.
Patrick **Lockheart** and Co. vs *James* **Estills** Administrators continued. Writ *Inquiry* set aside non ass *assume* within 5 years and Order.
John **Cline** vs *John* **McMahan** Dismissed.
Zachariah **Dozier** vs *Peter* **Evans** continued.
Robert **Brooks** vs *John* **Anderson** continued for plaintiff.
Patrick **Lockheart** vs *Thomas* **Welch** Continued.
Tucker administrators vs **Fenton** and **King** continued.
Philip **Philips** vs *Zachariah* **Dozier** Continued.
Christopher **Horn** vs *Jesse* **Hodges** judgment for £ 4-0-0 and costs. *Defendant did not appear so judgment awarded against him.*
Chins Executors vs *William* **Moore** continued for defendant.
Order that the Sherif pay to David **Lynch** and Harris **Massey** £ 12 part of the money due them for building the Courthouse.
John **Anderson** to pay John **Butler** and Thomas **Butler** for 2 day attendance against **Brooks**.
Weldon **South** to pay James **Callaway** for 4 days attendance and Traveling 32 miles and 3 Ferriges. Same to pay Edward **Fear** for one days attendance and Traveling 18 miles against **Grey**.
Christopher **Horn** to pay John **Johnson** 1 day attendance.
Same to pay David **Crews** 1 day attendance.
Same to pay Elizabeth **Long** 1 days attendance vs **Hodges**.
Order that James **Robertson** administrators of James **McNeely**, deceased pay to Michael **McNeely** and George **Adams** £ 25-8-0 guardians to the said James **McNeelys** orphans.
Ordered that Samuel **Estill** guardian to James **Estills** orphans be summoned to answer the complaint of Edward **Clark** for his freedom.

Order that the Court be adjourned untill Court in Course.
David **Gass**

At a Court held at Madison Courthouse on Tuesday the 23rd of December 1788.

Present David **Gass**, Archibald **Woods**, Joseph **Kennedy** and John **Miller**, gent.

Christopher **Harris** who was appointed to celebrate the rights of Marriages executed bond and took the oath prescribed by Law.

A State of the County Levy for 1788
To the Clerk for one year exoficio service 1500
To the Sheriff for the same 1500
To the State Attorney for the same 1500
To the Clerks for attending an exam Court on Jane
  and Rachel **Burton** [*Isaac* **Burton** *and ux*] 200
To the Sheriff for the same 200
To the Clerk for his service respecting the
  appointments of Commissioners 1000
To David **Lynch** and Harris **Massey** for building the
  Courthouse 13920
To Sherif for Commision for collecting 1177
To Depositions.. 4968
Credit by 828 tithes at 30# tobo...................... 24840

Ordered that Sherif pay William **Irvine** thirty three shillings for the purchase of the books to be paid out of the levy for 1787.

Order that Haile **Talbot** be appointed a Commissioner in room of John **Miller**.

Ordered that John **Snoddy** and David **Gass**, gent. be appointed to regulate the hands to work under James **Black**, Thomas **Campbell** and Thomas **Warren** and Boud **Estill** Surveyors of the road.

Order that the Court adjourn till Court in Course.
David **Gass**

Madison County, Kentucky Court Order Book A   51

At a Court continued and held at Madison Courthouse on Wednesday the 28th day Jan. 1789.

Present John **Snoddy**, David **Gass**, Archibald **Woods** and Joseph **Kennedy**, gent.

Joseph **Kennedy**, former Sheriff, took the oath of a Justice of the Peace whereupon he took his seat accordingly.

Commission was produced appointing John **Holly** and Charles **Debriel** to the office of Justices of the Peace in addition to those before appointed whereupon the said John **Holley** took the oaths prescribed by Law and took his seat Accordingly.

Ordered that the Sheriff pay James **French** thirty shillings out of the depositum for the purchase of two books for the use of his office.

Ordered that Archibald **Woods**, James **French** and John **Holly** be appointed to view and make report of the necessary alteration of the road from Taylors Fork to the Courthouse.

Present John **Miller**, gent.

John **Snoddy**, gent. procured a Commission from his Excellency appointing Sheriff of this County whereupon he took the Oath required by Law and entered into Bond Conditioned as the Law directs. George **Adams** and William **Irvine** his Security.

On motion of John **Snoddy**, gent., John **Gass** and William **Anderson** is appointed as Deputies whereupon they took the Oaths prescribed by Law.

George **Adams**, gent., former Sheriff, came into Court and took the oath of a Justice of Peace.

On motion of John **Snoddy** his Ear mark a crop and slit on the right Ear and under keel in the left ear is Ordered recorded.

John **Snoddy**, sheriff, came into Court and complained of the insuffiency of the jail in the County.

On the motion of John **Miller** his Ear mark a crop and two slits on the Left Ear is Ordered recorded.

Rates of Liquor and provision in this County.
Rum at two dollars per gallon.
Whiskey eight shillings for ditto.
Brandy ten shillings for ditto.

Beer two shillings per ditto.
Breakfast one shilling.
Supper the same.
Dinner one shilling and 3p.
Sixpence for lodging.
Nine pense For stable and hay or fodder for 12 hours for pasturage 18 hours 9 pense.
Corn and oats six pense per gallon.

Ordered that the Several Ordinary in this County do charge and receive in their respective Ordinarys agreable to the forgoing rates.
Ordered that James **French** surveyor of this County be admitted to transcribe his Recorder and that Aaron **Lewis** and John **Miller**, gent. be appointed to view his office and make report of same.
Order that the Court be adjourn until Court in Course.

George **Adams**

At a Court held at Madison Courthouse Tuesday the 3rd[*5th*] day of March 1789.
Present David **Gass**, Archibald **Woods**, Aron **Lewis** and John **Miller**, gent.

On motion of Jospeh **Butcher** his Ear mark a swaler fork in the left Ear is Ordered recorded.
Ordered that John **South** be permit to build a house on the Condemned Land and that he have leave to make use of the same so long as he Continues to retaile goods at the same and that he then return the house to this Court for the use and benefit of same.
Ordered that the Court be adjourned until Court in Course.

David **Gass**

At a Court held at Madison Courthouse on Tuesday the 7th day of April 1789.
Present George **Adams**, John **Boyles**, Robert **Rodes**, Bennett **Pemberton** and Moses **Dooley**, gent.

Madison County, Kentucky Court Order Book A			53

Order that Asaph **Walker**, Edward **Stephenson**, William **Morrison**, Philip **Williams** do view the road from the Kentucky River *near the mouth of Silver Creek* to where it may most Conveniently intersect the Road leading from Madison Courthouse to the Hazel Patch and make report.

A deed from Wallace **Estill** to Christopher **Harris** was proved by oaths of John **Woods** and William **Wallace** and ordered to be certified.

Ordered that George **Teter**, Jun. and Senr., Samuel **Harris** and George **Hinton** or any three of them be appointed to view a road from the Mouth of Back Creek to the mouth of Paint Lick Creek.

George **Adams**, guardian of James **McNeely**, *orphan of James McNeely Deceased* came into court and relinquished his guardianship for the said James **McNeely** whereupon the said James **McNeely** *being of lawful age* made choice of the said George **Adams** whereupon he entered into bond.

A deed from Thomas **Kennedy** to Richard **Runnals** was acknowledged and Ordered recorded.

A deed from James **Adams** to Joseph **Weldon** was acknowledged and Ordered recorded.

On the motion of Abraham **Buforder** a Ferry is establishd across the Kentucky River from or near the Mouth of Paint lick unto the opposite shore.

A deed from Ambrose and Hugh **Ross** and Gan [*Samuel*] **Haden** to Richard **Runnals** was acknowledged by Ambrose **Ross** as to the others proved by John **Boyle**, Dennis **Dover** and Ambrose **Ross** and Ordered recorded.

Order that the Court be adjourn till tomorrow 10 oclock.

George **Adams**

At a Court continued and held at Madison Courthouse on Wednesday the 8th day of April 1789.

Present George **Adams**, John **Boyles**, Archibald **Woods** and Moses **Dooley**, gent.

Ordered that John **Boyles** and Joseph **Kennedy**, Gent. be appointed to Settele with George **Adams**, gent. former Sheriff of the County and make a Report to the next Court.

Order that and Joseph **Kennedy**, gent. be appointed to divide the hands working on the road to Paint Lick from Silver Creek and from Back Creek to

Madison County, Kentucky Court Order Book A

where it intersects the road from the Courthouse and that William **Barnett** be appointed surveyor of the road from Paint Lick to Silver Creek in room of William **Morrison**.

Present David **Gass**, Joseph **Kennedy**, Aaron **Lewis** & Benett **Pemberton**, gent.

Joseph **Titus** vs John & Jesse **Helton** Continued at Defendant Costs.

Order that the rates crossing at the Ferry at the mouth of Paint Lick be as followeth for a man 3p and a horse the same and for the transport on of all other articles as Law directs.

Joseph **Titus** vs John **Helton** judgment confessed for 2 pounds and costs.

John **Phelps** vs William **Henry** judgment for three pounds.

Andrew **Vannoy** vs Jonathan **Longstreth** judgment per note.

Philip **Philips** vs Zach **Dozier** Continued.

Joseph **Butcher** vs John **Helton** and Joseph **Titus** judgment for 3 pounds.

The trustees for Harrodsburg vs *Barney* **Stagner**, James **Johnson** special bail.

Charles **Debriell**, gent. named in the Commission of the Peace for this County came into Court and took the oath of fidelity to the Commonwealth and the oath of a Justice of the Peace.

Present Charles **Dibrell**

David **Crews** and John **South** two of the inspectors appointed for **Boones** and **Collier** warehouses came into Court and took the oath of fidelity and oath of inspectors prescribed by Law and entered into bond as the Law directs.

Upon the motion of Michael **McNeally** an Injunction is granted him to stay proceedings on Judgment **Massie** against him by John **Adams** he giving bond as Law directs.

Ordered that the rules to be hereafter taken in the Clerks office shall be held on Wednesday next ensuing the first Tuesday in every month.

Upon the Motion of John **Holder** judgment is granted him against Aquila **White** upon Replevy bond. Legal notice being proved. *£ 3-6 and Costs.*

Order that the Court be adjourned till Court in Course.

Ordered that John **Hopkins** be appointed Constable in room of Michael **Farris**.

Ordered that the Court be adjourned until Court in Course.

George **Adams**

At a Court of Quarter Session held at Madison Courthouse Tuesday the 5th day of May 1789.

Present George **Adams**, David **Gass**, John **Boyles**, Archibald **Woods**, Joseph **Kennedy**, Benett **Pemberton** and Moses **Dooly**, gent.

Thomas **Kennedy**, foreman; Andrew **Kennedy**, James **Crawford**, Thymoly **Logan**, John **Bruse**, Joseph **Scott**, Henry **Wooly** [*Owley*], Samuel **Estill**, Green **Clay**, Higgason **Grubbs**, Joshua **McQueen**, John **Anderson**, Joshua **Barton**, Edward **Turner**, Edward **Williams**, Peter **Taylor**, Nicholas **Hawkins** and John **White** was sworn a Grand Jury for this County having Received their Charge retired to Consider their presentments.

Present Aaron **Lewis** and Robert **Rodes**, gent.

Order that Benett **Roberts** and John **Adams** be appointed Constables in this County.

A deed from the Executors of Richard **Henderson**, Deceased (*Bromfield Ridley, Robert Burton, Pleasant Henderson, Archibald Henderson, John Williams*) to Reubin **Searcy** was proved by the Oath Joseph **Moore** and Charles **Searcy** for 1000 acres of land with the courses annexed was Ordered Certified.

On the motion of Richard **Davis** a licence is granted him to keep tavern at This Courthouse whereupon he Entering into Bond Conditioned as the Law directs.

Commonwealth vs Samuel **Rice** plea filed rep*lications* dismissed.

Humphrey **Best** vs Thomas **Kennedy** continued.

William **Holland** vs Robert **Barton** dismissed.

Maurice **Nagle** vs *John* **Harris** Jury Sworn to Inquire of Damages towit. James **Stephenson**, John **Mitchel**, John **Mann**, Alexander **Reid**, Barney **Stagner**, John **Francis**, John **Pitman**, William **Robertson**, Thomas **Harris**, Samuel **Damon** [*Duncan*], Anthony **Roger** and Bazel **Maxwell** returned verdict for Plaintiff and judgment for £ 6-16-0.

James **Smith** vs *Aquilla* **White** dismissed agreed.

Robert **Burton** assee vs *John* **Phelps** judgment confessed for £ 11-9-0 with Interest from October 1787 untill paid.

The Grand Jury returnd presented the Surveyor of the road leading from Paint Lick forks of the road to the Crab Orchard also the survey from **Ham's** mill to the Tates Creek also Richard **Gorden** the surveyor of the road from

Sugar Creek to *Thomas* **Banks** and Jacob **Burgin** who is order to be summoned to answer to the same.

Benjamin **Brown** vs *Baptist* **Clark** continued.

John **Mitchel** vs *Green* **Clay** writ Inquiry set aside non assumd.

George **Teter** assee vs *Bartholomew* **Dawson**. Charles **Jones** common bail for the defendant delivered up the body of said **Dawson** whereupon he was prayed and ordered into the custody of the Sheriff and judgment for note confessed in custody.

William **Sprowl** vs *Joseph* **Scott** Issue waived and judgment for £ 20 and Interest from October 10, 1773.

George **Gray** vs *Weldon* **South** continued at Plaintiff Costs.

Weldon **South** to pay Flanders **Callaway** 4 days 54 miles and 7 Ferriges. Same to pay Edward **Fear** 1 day 18 miles 2 Ferriges. Same to pay William **Callaway** 5 day 54 miles 7 Ferriges. Same to pay James **Callaway** 1 day 36 miles and 2 Ferriges against **Gray**.

Robert **Brooks** vs John **Anderson** parties heard and dismissed at Plaintiff Costs.

John **Anderson** to pay Thomas **Butler** 2 day. Same to pay Philip **Butler** 1 day against **Brooks**.

Robert **Todd** vs *David* **Noble**. Thomas **Kennedy**, John **White** Special Bail.

Benjamin **Northcut** *by* George **Adams** vs *Luke* **Moore** Referred to James **McWhorter,** William **Finnell** and them umpire to arbitrate.

On the motion of Thomas **Harris** a Ferry Established across the Kentucky River at the Mouth of Sugar Creek on the upper sides thereof and that the rates of Ferriges be order for a man and for a horse the same.

Andrew **McKinley** vs *John* **Jackson** continued.

Order that the Court be adjourned tomorrow at 10 o'clock.

George **Adams**

At a Court Continued at Madison Courthouse on Wednesday the 6th day of May 1789.

Present George **Adams,** David **Gass,** John **Boyles,** Archibald **Woods** and Aaron **Lewis,** gent.

A deed from Stephen **Hancock** & *Kitty his wife* to Thomas **Hart** was acknowledged and Ordered recorded. And fem relinquished.

Ordered that the rates of retailing whiskey be as followeth 1/3 per point for all Quantities under a point or after that proportion and $1 above that in proportion for a greater or lessor Quantity.

Order that Samuel **Teter** be appointed Surveyor road from the mouth of Sugar Creek to **Banks** in the room of John **Mathews** and Moses **Dooley** be appointed to lott the tiths.

Patrick **Lockart** and Co vs *James* **Estill** administrators non Suit.

Present John **Miller**, gent.

Jeremiah **West** vs *Alexander* **Davis** *In Trespass Assault and Battery* set aside not guilty with Leave plead and non suit.

Commonwealth vs *Thomas* **Kennedy** Als.
Same vs *John* **Helton** continued.
Same vs *Adam* **Stear** *[Starnes]* dismissed.
Same vs *James* **Martin** continued.
Same vs *Joseph* **Merrit** continued.
Same vs *William* **Morrison** als.
Same vs *John* **Martin** continued.
Same vs *Jeremiah* **Perry** continued.
Same vs *Hugh* **Kilpatrick** continued.
Same vs *Joseph* **Scott** continued.
Same vs *John* **Pitman** continued.
James **Barnett** vs *Thomas* **Kennedy** continued.
Same vs Same Same.
Baptist **Clark** vs *Hugh* **Ross** continued.
Thomas **Kennedy** vs *Benjamin* **Proctor** continued.
Zachariah **Dozier** vs *Peter* **Evans** *Discontinued.*
Patrick **Lockhart** & Co. vs *Thomas* **Welch** continued.

Tucker administrators vs *Bartholomew* **Fentin** and *Aaron* **King** judgment for note. £ *3 with Interest from December 1786 and costs.*

Philip **Philips** vs *Zachariah* **Dozier** judgment for note. £ *1-18-1 and costs.*

Joseph **Titus** vs *John and Jesse* **Hiltons** judgment for £ 2-8-0 and costs.
Charles **Simpson** assee vs *James and Zachariah* **Dozier** continued.
William **Pawling** vs *Hugh* **Ross** judgment for £ 3-16-2 and costs.

James **Vaughn** vs *John* **Fitzgerald** judgment for £ 1-9-0 and costs.
Chins Executors vs *William* **Moore** continued.
Trustees of Harrodsburg vs *John* **Pitman** continued.
Jonathan **Owsley** vs *Baziel* **Maxwell** discontinued.
James **Dozier** vs *Ralph* **Morgan** dismissed Plaintiff costs.
James **Cowan** vs *David* **Noble** judgment for note and costs.
Charles **Dibriell** vs *William* **Holland** continued.
On the Motion of John **South**, Esquire License is granted him to keep a retail store at Madison Courthouse.
William **Gatlin** vs *William* **Mathews** continued.
Robert **Burton** vs *John* **Phelps** continued.
John **Cline** vs *Benjamin* **Williams** Als Sums.
Thomas **Parkham** vs *James* **Hogan** discontinued.
John **Mann** vs *Nicholas* **Proctor** continued.
Anthony **Rogers** vs *Hugh* **Ross** discontinued.
John **Adams** vs *Nicholas* **Proctor** Judgment confessed for £ 1-16-0 and costs.
Same vs **Deberell** Als Sums.
John **Adams** vs *John* **Anderson** continued.
John **Martin** assee vs *James* **French**. Writ of Inquiry set aside. Tender replicatn and Issue and Jury to try the same. Viz Robert **Deane**, Alexander **Davis**, Stephen **Hancock**, James **Hendricks**, Alexander **Kenny**, Joseph **Titus**, Matthew **Gwinn**, James I. **Dozier**, John **Adams**, David **Lynch**, Christopher **Harris**, and Reubin **Terrill**. Returned Verdict for Defendant new tryal on paying costs.
John **Mitchell** vs *Green* **Clay** Jury to try Issue. Viz Joseph **Brown**, David **Gentry**, William **Butcher**, Nicholas **Proctor**, James **Stephenson**, Henry **Leitch**, John **Reid**, Higgason **Grubbs**, William **Robertson**, Richard **Gordon**, Moses **Farris** and William **Howard**. Higgason **Grubbs** a juror withdrawn and the cause continued.
James **Martin** vs *John* **Kincaid** Jury to try Issue. Viz Robert **Dean**, Alex **Davis**, Stephen **Hancock**, James **Hendricks**, Alexander **Kenney**, Joseph **Titus**, Mathew **Guinn**, James I **Dozier**, John **Adams**, David **Lynch**, Christopher **Harris** and Reubin **Terrill**. Returned Verdict for Plaintiff for Debt to be discharged by 4 of Damages. Judgment new tryal on paying costs.

Madison County, Kentucky Court Order Book A

James **Martin** to pay Robert **Moor** 4 day. Same to pay William **Chennault** 4 day. Same to pay Thomas **Warren** 4 days vs **Kincaid**.
Clay to pay Thomas **Warren** 1 day against *John* **Mitchel**.
Martin to pay Nicholas **Proctor** 4 days.
Mitchel to pay Peter **Hacket** 5 days vs **Clay**.
John **Kinkaid** to pay John **Anderson** 2 day against of **Martin**.
John **Mitchel** to pay Samuel **Estill** 4 days. Same to pay Absolem **Hughs** 3 day vs **Clay**.
John **Kincaid** to pay Azariah **Martin** 1 day against **Martin**.

On the motion of Azariah **Martin** an injunction is granted him to stay all proceedings on a judgment obtained against him by Samuel **Coughran**.

On the motion of Thomas **Guest** an Injunction is granted him to stay all proceedings on judgment obtained against him by Edward **Williams** whereupon he Entered into bond Conditioned as the Law directs.

Ordered that the attorney for the County to commence a suit against Thomas **Crews** and his securities for a breach of their bond in not building and finishing the jail of this County.

Ordered that John **Kincaid** pay James **Stephenson** for two days Attendance as a Witness against **Martin** and also to pay Moses **Faris** for 2 days against *James* **Martin**.

Ordered that James **French** pay Higgason **Grubbs** two day attendance against *John* **Martin**.

Ordered that the Court be adjourned till Court in Course.
George **Adams**

At a Court held for Madison Courthouse on Tuesday the 2nd of June 1789.
Present George **Adams**, David **Gass**, Archibald **Woods**, Aaron **Lewis** and Charles **Debriel**, gent. Present Joseph Kennedy gent.

An Instrument of Writing from William **Kavanaugh** to Charles **Kavanaugh**, Senr. is acknowledged and ordered to be recordered.

A Deed from Wallace **Estill** to Christopher **Harris** is further proved by Oath of Joseph **Hancock** and Ordered to be Recorded.

A deed from David **Crews** to James **McDanil** is proved by the Oath of John **South** and Zedikiah **South** and is Orderd to be certified.

A deed from Thomas **Welch** to Archibald **Bell** is proved by the Oath of Aaron **Lewis** and James **McDaniel** and is Order to be Certified.

Order that this County be layed of into Districts as followeth for the Purpose of Electing overseers of the poor.

First Michael **McNeely** district as a Commissioner to be known by the name of the Paint Lick district and that William **Anderson** be appointed to Superintend the Election in the same at Thomas **Banks** on the 20th day of this Instant.

Second Haile **Talbot** district to be known by the name of Silver Creek and that John **Snoddy** be appointed to Superintend the election in the same on the 20th of this Instant and at Irvines Lick.

Third Aaron **Lewis** district to be known by the name of Tates Creek District and that John **Gass** be appointed to Superintend the Election the same at Green **Clay's** the 20th inst.

Ordered that Alex **Reed** be appointed surveyor in the room of Stephen **Hancock**.

Michael **McNeely** made satisfactory proof that he had served 19 days as a commissioner and that a certificate be granted him for same.

Order that John **Ship** [*Stepp*] be appointed Constabel in room of William **Holland**.

A deed from the executors of Richard **Henderson** (*John **Williams**, Bromfield **Ridley**, Robert **Burton**, Pleasant **Henderson**, Archibald **Henderson** and Elizabeth **Henderson**)* to Reubin **Searcy** was fully proved by the oath of Bennet **Searcy** and Ordered recorded.

Order that John **Harris** Sugar Creek, George **Yocum**, Samuel **Coughron**, John **Bolch**, John **Hisle** [*Harris*], Samuel **Gordon**, Uriah **Edwards** and Peter **Gater** be summond to appear at the next Court to Shew cause if any they can why they should not be fined and trible Taxed for not giving in their list of Taxable property acknowledged to Law.

Order that a Dedimus Issue to take the Deposition of Nicholas **Jones** and Ann **Bowers** in the suit Benjamin **Northcut** by his friend against Luke **Moore** in behalf of the debt.

On motion of Christopher **Owsley** and John **Adams** is appointed Guardian to John **Owley** orphan of John **Owley** Deceased and that appear at the next Court and give bond as the Law directs.

Present John **Miller** and Robert **Rodes**, gent.

Order that Asaph **Walker**, Philip **Williams**, William **Morrison** and Lofty **Pollins** be appointed to View the way for a road from John **Goggin** to where it may intersect the road leading from Paint Lick to Madison Courthouse and Edward **Stephenson**, Jasa [*Isaac*] **Anderson**, William **Miller** and Joseph **Kendy** *view the best way* from thence to where it may intersect the road leading from the Courthouse to Hazel Patch.

William **Irvine** produced a Commission from his Excellency the Governor appointing him Captain in the Malitia Cavalry for the County whereupon he took the Oaths prescribed by Law.

Samuel **South** produced a commission from his Excellency the appointing him Lieutenant in the Malitia Cavalry for this County whereupon he took the Oaths prescribed by Law.

A deed and Coms from William **Hays** and *Susannah his* wife to John **Holley** was proved by the Oaths of Samuel **Estill** and Samuel **South** and Order to be Certified.

Ordered that Joseph **Kennedy**, gent. be recommended to his Excellency the Governor as a proper person to Commission as a Major in this County.

Ordered that Mathew **Adams** be recommended to his Excellency the Governor as a proper person to Commission as Captain in the Militia in this County. Also Andrew **Miller** as Lieutenant and Robert **Kincaid** as Ensign.

A deed from Samuel **Davis** and *Jane his wife* to Benjamin **Morton** was acknowledged and ordered to be Recorded.

A deed from Samuel **Davis** and *Jane his wife* to Alexander **McKay** was acknowledged and ordered to be recorded.

A deed from Samuel **Davis** and *Jane his wife* to George **Wolfscale** was acknowledged and ordered to be recorded.

A deed from Samuel **Davis** and *Jane his wife* to David **Shelton** was acknowledged and ordered to be Recorded.

Ordered that Jonathan **Owley**, George [*David*] **Fenley** and William **Morrison** be recommended as Captains.

On the motion and oath a didmus is granted Baptist **Clark** to take the deposition of John **Francis** Do be assee against of **Brown**.

Ordered that John **Frances**, John **Black**, Moses **Dooley** and Benjamin **Cooper** be recommended to his Excellency as Lieutenant and William **Small**, William **McClure**, William **Anderson** and Richard **Callaway** as Ensigns.

Ordered that John **Owsley** be permitted to build a mill on Sugar Creek being his own Land on both sides of said creek.

Ordered that the Sheriff may receive a Receipt from any white tithe in this County from Harris **Massie** or David **Lynch** two shillings and one penny which shall be considered as part of his County levey for the year 1788.

A deed from Higgason **Grubbs** and *Lucy his wife* to Edward **Turner** is acknowledged feme before relinquished and Order to be Recorded.

Ordered that Bennett **Searcy**, Esqr. be recommended to the Honorable the Judges of the Supreme Court of the District of Kentucky as a person of Honesty, Probity and Good Demeanor for the purpose of Obtaining a lisence to practice as an attorney in the County and other Inferior Courts.

Samuel **Rice** vs Denis **Diver** atth continued.

Ordered that it be Certified to his Excellency the Governor that this Court Call on John **Snoddy**, Sheriff of this County for Bond Security for the Collection of the revenue Tax and he refused to give Security for the same and that David **Gass** and James **Barnett** stands first in the Commission of the peace and are proper person to fill up that Commission.

The Sheriff of this County returnd a pole of the election of Trustees for Town of Boonsborough which was Ordered to be recorded.

Ordered that Thomas **Kennedy**, John **Goggin**, James **French**, Samuel **Estill**, John **Kincaid**, James **Anderson**, Green **Clay** and John **Adams** be recommended to his Excellency the Governor as propper person to be added to the Commissions of the peace.

Order that the Court adjourn till Court in Course.

George **Adams**

A Court Called and held and at Madison Courthouse on Monday the 27th day of June 1789 for the Examination of Charles **Hucherson** charged with feloniously murdering Baptist **Clark** before the worshipfull of George **Adams**, David **Gass**, John **Boyles**, Archibald **Woods**, Joseph **Kennedy**, Aron **Lewis**, Robert **Rodes**, Moses **Dooly**, John **Miller** and Charles **Dibriel**. The said Charles **Hucherson** was led to the bar and heard in his own defense whereupon sundry witnesses were sworn and examined on behalf of the Commonwealth. It is the opinion of This Court that he be acquited and discharged from the Charge aforesaid the Court then disolved.

George **Adams**

Madison County, Kentucky Court Order Book A 63

At a court held at Madison Courthouse on Tuesday the 17th day of July 1789. Present George **Adams**, Archibald **Woods**, Joseph **Kennedy** and Charles **Debriel**, gent.

A Power attorney from Samuel **Dawson** to Thomas **Dawson** is acknowledged and Ordered to be recorded.

Present Bennett **Pemberton** and Moses **Dooley**, gent.

Orderd that John **Boyles**, Michael **McNeely**, James **Henderson** and George **Adams** be appointed Commissioners to alott and to David **Hogan** on behalf of his wife Elizabeth **Hogan** formerly Elizabeth **Owley** widow to John **Owley**, Deceased her dower of the Estate of the said John **Owley**, Deceased.

A power of attorney from John **Hiatt** to Thomas **Gist** was proved by the oaths of Bennett **Pemberton** and is Ordered to be Recorded.

A deed from David D **Maxwell** and *Mary his wife* to John **Brown** together with a Memo thereon was acknowledged femme relinquished her right of Dower and Ordered recorded.

A deed from Thomas **Welch** to Archibald **Bell** was fully proved by the Oath of John **Collier** and Ordered recorded.

Present Robert **Rodes**, gent.

Bartholomew **Dawson** an Insolvent debtor at the Suit of George **Teter** having remained in Jail for twenty days was brought into Court pursuant to a warrant Issued by Joseph **Kennedy**, gent who delivered in a Schedule of his Estate and took the oath of an Insolvent Debtor and is discharged out of Custody.

Letters of administrator is Granted to John **Alcorn** on the Estate of James **Alcorn**, Deceased who together with Jonathan **Owsley** his security Entered into bond Conditioned as the Law Directs.

Ordered that George **Adams**, Moses **Dooley**, William **Wallace** and John **Mounce** or any three of them being first Sworn do appraise the Estate of James **Alcorn**, Deceased.

Baptist **Clark** vs *Hugh* **Ross** abates by Plaintiffs death.

Ordered that James **Turner**, Joseph **Proctor**, Andrew **Woods** and John **Woods** be appointed to view the most convenient way for a road from **Woods** Station to the forks of the Road about a mile Southeast of Edward **Turners** and make Report thereof to the next September Court.

Thomas **Kennedy** vs *Benjamin* **Proctor** continued.

Lockart & Co vs *Thomas* **Welch** continued.
Chinn's executors vs *William* **Moore** continued.
Andrew **McKinley** vs *John* **Jackson** discontinued with costs.
Charles **Simmons** *assee* vs *James and Zachariah* **Dozier** continued.
Trustees of Harrodsburg vs *John* **Pitman** judgment confess off Act.
John **Jackson** to pay Nancy **Harris** for two days.
Same to pay Robert **Harris** same.
Same to pay William **Hancock** for 1 day.
Same to pay John **Jackson** for 2 days attendance 25 Miles against *Andrew* **McKinley**.
Andrew **McKinley** to pay Marvel **Nash** 2 days and 25 Miles. Same to pay Jesse **Emmerson** 2 days and 25 Miles vs *John* **Jackson**.
William **Gatlin** vs *William* **Mathews** continued.
Robert **Burton** vs *John* **Phelps** dismissed.
John **Phelps** to pay John **Phelps** Jr. 1 days attendance. Same to pay William **Harris** Ditto. Same to pay Cary **Phelps** Ditto against *Robert* **Burton**.
John **Man** vs *Nicholas* **Proctor** continued.
John **Adams** vs *Charles* **Deberill** judgment confessed for £ 1-16 and costs.
Same vs *John* **Anderson** continued.
Jonathan **Owsley** vs *Israel* **Harmon** continued.
William **Bledsoe** vs *James* **Shackelford** judgment confessed for costs.
Same vs Same Same.
Same vs *Henry* **Yater** Same.
Same vs Same Same.
Arthur **Moore** vs *Benjamin* **Northcut** *by George Adams, Jr.* continued.
John **Adams** to pay Allen **Burton** 1 day attendance vs *Charles* **Debrell**.
Andrew **Hare** vs *William* **Harris** continued.
Jesse **Robards** vs *James* **Cosgrove** judgment for £ 1-10-0.
William **Dryden** vs *Thomas* **Reynolds** Als.
Green **Clay** vs *William* **Sutherland** continued.
Samuel **Rice** vs *Dennis* **Devers** continued.
William **Hoy** vs *Charles* **Debriell** continued at Plaintiff Costs.
James **French** vs *William* **Hoy** Als.
Dibriell vs **Holland** als.

Ordered that Edward **Taylor**, Thomas **Tipton**, Stout **Brinson** and Carry **Phelps** do View a way for a road from *William* **Ham's** Mill to near *Bartholomew* **Finton's** on the road to Danville.

A report of an amendment to the road from Taylor Fork to the Courthouse is Established and it is Ordered that Surveyor open the same Accordingly.

Order that the Court adjourn until Court in Course.

George **Adams**

At a Court of Quarter Session held at Madison Courthouse on Tuesday the 4th day of August 1789.

Present George **Adams**, David **Gass**, Archibald **Woods**, Joseph **Kennedy**, Robert **Rodes** and John **Miller**, gent.

Thomas **Kennedy**, foreman; Isaac **Williams**, Benjamin **Okley**, Dotson **Thorpe**, Joel **Hill**, Leonard **Hetherly**, Charles **Ballew**, Edward **Williams**, Stephen **Hancock**, Robert **Henderson**, Humphrey **Best**, Alex **Reed**, William **Miller**, John **Anderson**, James **Crawford**, Andrew **Kennedy** and Samuel **Gorden** were sworn a Grand Jury for the body of this County having received their charge retired to consider of their presentments.

Present Joseph **Kennedy**, gent.

Commonwealth vs *James* **Henderson** Continued.

George **Grey** vs *Weldon* **South** discontinued with Costs.

Benjamin **Brown** vs *Baptist* **Clark** abates by Defendants Death.

John **Martin** assee vs *James* **French** Jury sworn to try the Issue towit. Robert **Henry**, Jeremiah **Perry**, Benjamin **Cooper**, Sam **Teter**, George **Finley**, James **Howard**, Jesse **May**, Sharwell **Cooper**, William **Powel**, Andrew **Harris**, James **Matthews** and George **Teter** returned verdict for Plaintiff Damage for £ 5-3-6 and Judgment.

Weldon **South** to pay Flanders **Callaway** 1 day 18 miles. Same to pay Edward **Fear** one day 18 Miles and Ferriage. Same to pay William **Callaway** same vs **Grey**.

John **Martin** came into Court and acknowledged that he released Alex **Maxwell** and Benjamin **Johnson** from all obligation of a note assee by them on James **French** or right of action in above suit.

The Grand Jury returned and presentment the Surveyor of the Road from John **Woodruff** to William **Handcocks** also the Surveyor of the road from

Henderson to Samuel **Rice's** also the surveyor of the road from *William* **Miller** to *Thomas* **Kennedy's** and the surveyor from Tates Creek to the fork of the Boonsborough road and they are ordered to be summon to answer to the same *for not keeping their several roads in repair.*

John **Martin** to pay Alexander **Maxwell** 1 days attendance and 30 Miles.

Same to pay Benjamin **Johnson** the same vs *James* **French**.

Cary **Phelps** vs *David* **Kennedy** dismised the Defendants Costs.

John **Mitchell** vs *Green* **Clay** Jury to try Issue towit. James I. **Dozier**, Peter **Evans**, Samuel **Boyd**, John **Kincaid**, William **Williams**, Abraham **Boyd**, Peter **Woods**, Charles **Kavanaugh**, William **Handcock**, William **McGuire**, Joseph **Butcher**, Samuel **Coughran**. Returned verdict for Plaintiff £ 23 Damages.

An instrument of writing from Samuel **Ewing** to William **Hoy** was proved by the oath of William **Miller** and Ordered recorded.

James **French** vs *William* **Hoy** dismissed at Defendants Costs.

Mark **Ozburn** vs Henry **Wells** dismissd.

Enoch **Tucker** administrators (*Harry* **Innes**) vs *Aaron* **King** *and John Dyer* Issue waved and Judgment & spe. *£ 3 with interest from December 1786.*

James **Barnett** vs *Thomas* **Kennedy** continued.

Same vs Same Same.

Thomas **Kennedy** vs *James* **Barnett** continued.

Northcutt and als. *by his friend George Adams* vs Luke **Moore**. Arther **Moore** Special Bail.

Fredericks **Rapidan** vs *William* **Simpson** continued.

John **Holder** vs *William* **Hoy** continued.

Andrew **Dods** vs *Alexander* **Kenney** Jury sworn to try Damages William **Robinson** [*Robertson*], Nicholas **Hawkins**, Joseph **Titus**, John **Helten**, Robert **Kilpatrick**, Thomas **Warren**, William **Barnett**, William **Terel**, Isaac **Pattern**, James **Anderson**, William **Woods** and John **Cochran** returned verdict for the Plaintiff £ 8-0-1 damage and judgment.

William **Hoy** vs *Charles* **Dibrell** dismissed at defendants costs.

Green **Clay** to pay Thomas **Warren** 1 day vs *John* **Mitchell**.

Order that Court adjourn tomorrow 9 o'clock.

George **Adams**

Madison County, Kentucky Court Order Book A 67

At a Court continued and held at Madison Courthouse on Wednesday the 5th day of August 1789.

Present George **Adams**, David **Gass**, Archibald **Woods** and John **Miller**, gent.

On motion of James **French** a new trial is granted him against *John* **Martin** on payment of costs.

Giles **Tompkins** was nominated by James **French** as a Deputy Surveyor. Ordered that James **Barnett** and Thomas **Reynolds** examine into his capacity and ability to discharge the said office.

Present Joseph **Kennedy** and Robert **Rodes**, gent.

Patrick **Gallihar** vs *John* **Martin** jury to inquire &c Viz Thomas **Campbell**, Joseph **Pitman**, William **Morrison**, Whison **George**, Achilles **Hughbank**, William **Orear**, David **Lynch**, John **Campbell**, James **Crawford**, Robert **Henry**, William **Robertson**, James **French** and returned verdict for the plaintiff £ 5 damages.

James **Barnett** and Thomas **Reynolds** appointed to examine Giles **Thomkins** reported him duly qualified whereupon the said Giles took the oaths of office.

Best vs **Kennedy** discontinued for plaintiff.

James **Martin** vs *John* **Kincaid** discontinued agreed.

John **Sydbottom** vs *Bennett* **Roberts** same.

William **Pollard** vs *Ralph* **Morgan**. Jury sworn to Inquire viz Michael **McNeely**, James **Black**, Robert **Henderson**, James **Howard**, John **Hopkins**, John **Mitchell**, Joseph **Moore**, Andrew **Donaldson**, Barney **Stagner**, William **Kincaid**, Samuel **Estill** and John **Harper** returned verdict for the plaintiff £ 7 damages and Judgment.

Ordered that Edmund **Terrill** be recommended to his Excellency the Governor as a proper person to be commissioned as Captain in the Militia in this County also James **Finnell** as Lieutenant and Hardy **Bennett** as Ensign.

Ordered that John **Martin** be fined the sum of five pounds for contempt to this Court.

Samuel **Estill** special bail in the room of James I. **Dozier** in the suit *Jesse* **Hodges** *assee* vs Zach **Dozier**.

Jesse **Hodges** asse vs *Zachariah* **Dozier** Jury sworn to try Issue Viz. James **Black**, Robert **Henderson**, James **Howard**, John **Harper**, John

Hopkins, William Kincaid, James Moore, John Mitchell, Andrew Donalson, Abraham Boyd, Jeremiah Perry and Barney Stagner returned verdict for the defendant.

William Pollard to pay John Clark two days vs Morgan.

Samuel Rice vs Dennis Devers judgment for £ 3 and goods attached to be sold and Ordered sale.

John Mitchell to pay Peter Hack [Hackett] two days vs Green Clay.

Harry Innes assee vs Higgason Grubbs. James French special bail.

Zachariah Dozier to pay Thomas Butler 2 days. Same to pay Joseph Merritt 2 days. Same to pay Isaac Burgin 2 days against Hodges.

Patrick Galliher to pay Dennis Cochran 1 day vs Martin.

Green Clay vs William Southerland. Robert Henderson garnishee confessed on oath that he had a negro boy the property of William Southerland. Judgment is granted the plaintiff for £ 7-9-6 and costs and order of sale for the attached property as confessed.

Thomas Kennedy vs Benjamin Proctor judgment on note £ 2-2.

Patrick Lockheart vs Thomas Welch continued.

Chinn's executors vs William Moore continued for defendant.

Benjamin Northcut vs Luke Moore order reference set aside.

Charles Dibrile vs William Holland discontinued.

William Gatlin vs William Matthews a judgment £ 2-10-6 and costs.

John Mann vs Nicholas Proctor judgment for £ 30 and costs.

John Adams vs John Anderson continued.

Andrew Hare vs William Harris continued.

Charles Simpson asee vs Zachariah Dozier discontinued agreed.

John Adams assee vs William Hopper dismissed.

Andrew Johnson claims 2 days and traveling 30 miles in the suit Mann vs Nicholas Proctor.

Zachariah Dozier to pay James I. Dozier 2 day attendance against Jesse Hodges.

Jonathan Owsley vs Israel Harmon continued for defendant.

Fitzgerald vs Knox all sum 5.

William Dryden vs Thomas Reynolds continued.

Arthur Moore asee vs Benjamin Northcut and George Adams continued untill the suit Northcutt vs Moore is tried.

John Cline vs Benjamin Williams continued.

Samuel **Estill** claims 1 day in the suit *John* **Mitchell** vs *Clay*. **Mitchell** to pay same.

John **Courtney** vs *Israel* **Harmon** continued.
Charles **Campbell** vs *Humphrey* **Best** continued.
James **French** vs *William* **Hoy** continued.
Elijah **Gaddy** vs *Joseph* **Merit** discontinued.
Thomas **Southerland** vs *Nicholas* **Proctor** continued.
Bennett **Smith** vs *Edward* **Williams** continued.

On the motion of James **Barnett** a Dedimus is awarded him to take deposition of William **Cabell**, Sr. and John **Barnett**--Amherst County vs **Kennedy**.

On the oath of Humphrey **Best** a dedimus is awarded him to take deposition of Joseph **Weldon** against Charles **Campbell**.

George **Adams**, David **Gass**, James **Barnett**, Archibald **Woods**, Robert **Rodes** and Joseph **Kennedy** took the oaths prescribed and required by the act of Congress if their act the 1st of June 1789. John **Snoddy**, William **Irvine** and James **French** took the oath.

On the oath of Robert **Dean** a Dedimus is awarded him to take the deposition of Joseph **McKinney** against **Kennedy**.

Ordered that the sheriff do have the necessary repairs done to the goal of this County.

Ordered that James **Barnett**, gent. be appointed to assist the persons before appointed to settle with the former sheriff and make report to the next Court.

John **Miller**, gent. took the oath required by the Congress of the United States.

Ordered that the Court adjourn till Court in Course.

George **Adams**

At a Court held at Madison Courthouse Tuesday 2nd day of September 1789.
Present George **Adams**, John **Boyle**, Archibald **Woods**, Joseph **Kennedy** and John **Miller**, gent.

John **Boyle**, gent. took the oath required by the Congress of the United States.

Ordered that John **Collier** and Richard **Runnolds** be exempted from paying County Levy.

Ordered that Jesse **Embry** be exempted from paying one County levy for the year 1788.

A power of attorney from Edward **Logsdon** and *Mary his wife* to Richard **Mill** was acknowledged and Ordered recorded.

A deed from Joseph **Kennedy** and *Patsy his wife* to Andrew **Harris** was acknowledged and Ordered recorded. feme relinquished.

Ordered that Jesse **Cofer**, David **Wilcocks**, William **Williams** and David **Hall** be appointed to review the way for road at the mouth of Tates Creek.

Ordered that the heirs of William **Vancleave**, Edward **Taylor**, Abraham **Buford** and *Giles* **Tompkins** be summoned to appear before the next Court to shew if they have any objection to a road going through their lands.

Ordered that Thomas **Banks** be appointed surveyor of the road from the forks *of the Sugar Creek road* to William **Poes** and Samuel **Teter** thence on to the mouth of Sugar Creek and M. **Dooley** to lott tithes.

A deed and commission from William **Hoy** and *Sarah his wife* to John **White** was acknowledged and Ordered recorded.

Ordered that John **Campbell** be appointed surveyor of the road in room of Thomas **Campbell**.

A deed from William **Robertson** and *Sarah his wife* to John **Pitman** *and Dorotha his wife* was acknowledged by **Robertson** and Ordered recorded.

An instrument of writing from William **Allen** to Alexander **Duglas** was acknowledged by the oath of William **Hows** and ordered recorded.

Ordered that *Irvine* ***Jones*** *be appointed Surveyor* of the road in *the room of John **Woodrooff*** also ordered that Thomas **Turner** in the room of Thomas **Baker**.

William **Irvine**, Clerk of this Court made oath to an *Statement* of his fees which is ordered to be Certifyed.

A Deed from Robert **Henderson** to Alexander **Reid** was acknowledged and ordered recorded.

A report of Road from **Wood's** Station to the forks of the road *Southeast of Edward* **Turner's** is Established. Andrew **Woods** Surveyor *of said road* and Archibald **Woods**, gent to lott the tithes.

On the motion of Thomas **Kennedy** a dedimus is granted him to take the deposition of Azariah **Martin** debeniesse against of James **Barnett**.

On the motion of Robert **Adams** a dedimus is granted him to take the deposition of Andrew **Miller** debenesse for against of **Weldon** and ux.

A deed from William **Jones** and *Mary his wife* to Irvine **Jones** was acknowledged and ordered recorded. Feme Relinquished.

A deed from William **Dryden** and *Mary his wife* to John **Cochran** was acknowledged and ordered recorded.

A deed from William **Dryden** and *Mary his wife* to Cornelius **Daugherty** was acknowledged and ordered recorded.

George **Hart** being nominated as a Deputy Surveyor for this County ordered that John **Adams** and James **Anderson** do examine into his fitness and Capacity to execute the said office and report.

Patrick **Lockheart** and Co. vs. *Thomas* **Welch** Dismissed at Plaintiff Costs. £ 3 *and costs.*

Chinn's Executors vs *William* **Moore**. Parties heard and judgment for £ and costs.

John **Adams** vs *John* **Anderson** discontinued.

The examiners appointed to examine George **Hart** was this day nominated to the office of a Deputy Surveyor in this County returned this report that he was capable to execute the said office whereupon he took the oath of Fidelity, the oath to the United States, the Oath of Office.

Andrew **Hare** vs *William* **Harris** continued.

William **Dryden** vs *Thomas* **Reynolds** continued.

John **Cline** vs *Benjamin* **Williams** continued for defendant.

A deed from William **Hoy** and *Sarah his wife* to Green **Clay** was acknowledged by the said William and Ordered to be Recorded.

Jonathan **Owsly** vs *Israel* **Harman**. Judgment £ 2-8-0 *and costs.*

On the motion and affidavit of William **Hoy** a Dedimus is awarded him to take the Depositions of Thomas **Chiles**, George **Davidson**, William **Threadgile**, Francis **Smith**, William **Rickett** and Thomas **Higgenson** of Anson County North Carolina against *James* **Hogan**.

Cary **Phelps** vs *Daniel* **Hix**. Judgment confessed for Costs.

Deed from John **Tanner** and *Rachel his wife* to James **Hendricks** acknowledged and Feme Relinquished and ordered recorded.

Deed from William **Dryden** and Mary his wife to John **Snoddy** acknowledged by the said William and ordered to be recorded.

Deed from William **Montgomery** to John **Cochran** was acknowledged and was proved by the oaths of James **Barnett** and James **Anderson** and Ordered Certified.

Commonwealth vs *Joseph* **Merritt** Judgement for 5 *shillings* and Costs.
Same vs John **Martin** Same. Same.
Same vs *Jeremiah* **Perry** Same. Same.
Same vs *Hugh* **Kilpatrick** Same. Same.
Same vs *Joseph* **Scott** Same. Same.
Same vs *Thomas* **Kennedy** Same. Same.
Same vs *John* **Pitman** dismissed.
Same vs *Jacob* **Burgin** judgment for 5 *shillings* and costs.
Same vs *Richard* **Gordon** Same. Same.
Same vs *William* **Ham** Same for 15 *shillings* and costs.
Same vs *James* **Henderson** dismissed.

Ordered that Richard **Runnols** extend his road as far as Robert **Henderson's** and James **Henderson** appointed surveyor of the Danville Road from Back Creek to the forks of the Crab Orchard Road and John **Boyles**, gent. to alot the tithes.

Commonwealth vs *John* **Mathew** continued.

William **Ham** to pay Thomas **Kennedy** 1 day attendance against Commonwealth.

On the motion of James **Barnett** a dedimus is granted to take the deposition of Thomas **Morrison** vs *Thomas* **Kennedy**.

Bennett **Smith** vs *Edward* **William** judgment £ 3-0-0 *and costs*.

A deed from Robert **Henderson** and *Franky his wife* to John **Brown** was acknowledged and Ordered recorded. Feme relinquished.

John **Fitzjorel** vs *Thomas* **Knox** dismissed.
Charles **Campbell** vs *Humphrey* **Best** at plaintiffs cost continued.
John **Harris** assee vs *James* **Martin** *and John* **Miller** dismissed.
Higgason **Grubbs** vs *Robert* **Rodes** dismissed.
John **Cortney** vs *Israel* **Harmon** continued.
Jacob **Stearns** vs *Thomas* **Owden** als.

Ordered that John **Adams** be appointed a Commissioner in the room of Michael **McNeely**.

James **French** vs *William* **Hoy** continued.
John **Jones** vs *William* **McCollough** continued.

Ordered that William **Jones**, David **Crews** and John **South** be recommended as inspectors at Boonsborough and **Colliers**.

A deed and Commission from William **Hays** and *Susannah his wife* to John **Holly** was fully proved by the oath of John **Wilkerson** and Ordered recorded.

Ordered that the Court adjourn until Court in Course.

George **Adams**

At a Court *of Quarter Sessions* held for Madison County on Tuesday the 6th day of October 1789.

Present George **Adams**, David **Gass**, John **Boyles** and Joseph **Kennedy**, gent.

Moses **Dooley**, gent. took the oath required by the United States.

John **Reid**, Esqr. produced a license to practice as an attorney whereupon he took the oath required by Law.

Heziah **Crampton** vs *Aaron* **King**. Thomas **Hall** security for costs.

Thomas **Kennedy**, foreman; William **Handcock**, Samuel **Freeman**, Edward **Turner**, Jeremiah **Crews**, John **White**, Leon **Hetherly**, Zack **Dozier**, John **Woodruff**, Robert **Henderson**, Cornelius **Daugherty**, Samuel **Gordon**, Andrew **Kennedy**, Alex **Reed**, John **Kincaid**, Humphrey **Best** sworn a Grand Jury retired.

A deed John **Jackson** and *Elizabeth his wife* to William **Holland** acknowledged and ordered recorded. fem relinquished.

Absent George **Adams**, gent. Present James **Barnett**, gent.

On the motion of William **Pollard** a judgment is granted him vs Ralph **Morgan** and Joseph **Turner** for the sum of £ 11-3-4½ for not delivering property agreeable to their bond, notice being proved.

A deed and Commission from William **Hoy** and *Sarah his wife* to Green **Clay** returned and order to be recorded being before acknowledged.

Andrew **Hare** vs *William* **Harris** referred to John **Hunter** and George **Elliott** their umpire.

The Grand Jury returned and presented the surveyor of the road from William **Hancocks** to the Courthouse who is ordered sarne.

Deed from Richard **Walker** to David **Wells** acknowledged and Ordered recorded.

On motion of Elizabeth **Turpin** letters of administration is granted her on the estate of Solomon **Turpin** whereupon she entered into bond and took the oath required by Law. *Securities are Higgason* **Grubbs** *and George* ***Boon****.*

Ordered that Edward **Turner**, Robert **Moore**, Jesse **Embry**, Jesse **Noland** or any three of them appraise the estate of Solomon **Turpin** and report.

Deed from Samuel **Davis** and *Jane his wife* to Richard **Gentry** acknowledged & ordered Recorded.

Same to David **Gentry** Same and Ordered recorded.

Same to Micajah **Farris** Same Same.

Same to David **Shelton** (fem relinquished) and being before acknowledged & Ordered recorded.

Same to George **Wolfscale**--Same--

Same to Alex **McKay** Same.

Same to David **Gass** Same.

Robert **Adams** appeared according to the condition of his recognance for giving security for the maintanence of a bastard child begotten on the body of Phebe **Best** now Phebe **Weldon**; On consideration of the matter it is ordered that the same be continued until the next Court.

Robert **Adams** recognized in the penalty of £ 10 to appear at and abide by the order of the next Court.

Commonwealth vs *George* **Boon** dismissed.

John **Martin** asee vs *James* **French** judgment confessed for £ 5-2-0 and costs.

Commonwealth vs *Robert* **Moore** dismissed.

A deed Samuel **Davis** and ux to John **Hill** acknowledged and Ordered recorded. Fem relinquished.

Commonwealth vs *Richard* **Ronnalds** dismissed.

Same vs *Samuel* **Rice** continued.

Same vs *John* **Holton** continued.

Same vs *James* **Martin** continued.

Same vs *William* **Morrison** continued.

Same vs *John* **Mathews** judgment for 15 *shillings* and costs.

Samuel **Estill** and Charles **Cavanaugh** produced Commissions appointing them Captains in the Militia of this County who severally took the oath of Fidelity.

Commonwealth vs *James* **Hendricks** dismissed.
Same vs *Samuel* **Woods** continued.
Report of a road from John **Goggins** to Edward **Stephenson** was returned and ordered to record.
William **Orear** qualified as Deputy Sheriff and took the oath to support the Constitution of the United States.
Ordered that John **Goggin**, overseer of the road from **Goggins** to the Wolfpen, Nicholas **Hawkins** from the Wolfpen to where the road crosses Paint Lick Road, Joseph **Scotts** from thence to **Stephenson**.--George **Adams** and Joseph **Kennedy** to allott the tithes.
James **Anderson** nominated as Deputy Surveyor. James **Barnett** and William **Orear** appointed to examine him; who found him duly qualified and the said James took the oath of office.
Ordered that Thomas **Kennedy**, John **Boyles**, David **Kennedy** and Robert **Kincaid** do view the most convenient way for a road from Thomas **Bradley's** to the Round Stone Lick and make report.
James **Barnett** vs *Thomas* **Kennedy** continued.
Same vs Same Same.
Thomas **Kennedy** vs *James* **Barnett** Same.
William **Bush** vs *John* **Holly** Same.
Frederick **Ripardon** vs *William* **Simpson** same.
Trustees &c vs *Barney* **Stagner**. Issue waived and judgment by nonsom. £ 5 and costs.
Hezekiah **Crumpton** vs *Aaron* **King** continued.
John **Holder** vs *William* **Hoy** continued.
Abraham **Burton** vs *William* **Orchard** continued.
Simon **Gentry** vs *Jeremiah* **Parks** same.
James **Hogan** vs *William* **Hoy** same.
Samuel **Hopper** *by William* **Hopper** *his father* vs *Samuel* **Bickerstaffe** same.
William **Dryden** vs *Thomas* **Reynolds** continued.
John **Clyne** vs *Benjamin* **Williams** dismissed.
Charles **Campbell** vs *Humphrey* **Best** continued.
James **French** vs *William* **Hoy** dismissed.
John **Cortney** vs *Israel* **Harmon** continued.
Thomas **Sutherland** vs *Nicholas* **Proctor** continued.

John **Jones** vs *William* **McCullough** same.
Jacob **Starns** vs *Thomas* **Owden** continued.
John **Phelps** vs *Robert* **Burton** continued.
John **Miller** vs *John* **Adams** &c. als sums.
Ordered that the Court be adjourned till Court in Course.

George **Adams**

At a Court held for Madison County on Tuesday the 3rd day of November 1789.

Present John **Boyles**, Archibald **Woods**, Joseph **Kennedy** and Moses **Dooley**, gent.

Aron **Lewis**, gent. took the oath required by the Congress of the United States.

An inventory and appraisement of the Estate of Solomon **Turpin**, deceased returned and ordered recorded.

A Power of attorney from Dennis **Dever** to John **Boyles** was proved by the oaths of Joseph **Montgomery** and James **Kennedy** and Ordered recorded.

On the motion of John **Boyles** Letters of administration is granted him on the estate of Denis **Dever**, Deceased whereupon he entered into bond and took the oath required by Law. *Security is John* **Snoddy**.

A deed from John **Bryant** attorney in fact for George **Smith** to John **McLean** was acknowledged and Ordered recorded.

A deed from James **Mason** and *Elizabeth his wife* to John **Patterson** was acknowledged and Ordered recorded and feme relinquished.

Order that David **Hall** be appointed surveyor of the road in room of George **Boone**, and John **Jackson** be appointed surveyor in the room of Thomas **Baker**.

Order that Robert **Moore**, Edward **Turner**, Jesse **Embry** and Jesse **Noland** be appointed to lott of the dower of Elizabeth **Turpen** widow of Solomon **Turpin** Deceased.

On the motion of Peter **Taylor** his ear mark a crop and two slits in the rights and a hole in the left ear is O.R.

On motion of William **Chennault** his ear mark a crop and a slit in the right and an under keel in the left ear is Ordered recorded.

A Power of attorney from Boud **Estill** to Wallace **Estill** was acknowledged. and Ordered recorded.

Commonwealth vs Samuel **Woods** [PP written above Woods] dismissed. Memo and receipt.

Deed from Robert **Henderson** to Joseph **Horn** acknowledged and Ordered recorded.

Humphrey **Best** surveyor of road from Paint Lick to **Hendersons**. Robert **Branks** on from thence to the County line in the room of Samuel **Woods**. George **Adams**, gent. to allot the tithes.

Thomas **Kennedy**, George **Adams**, William **Bartlett**, Henry **Wooley** or any 3 to review the road from the **McLeod's** fort to the mouth of Sugar Creek and report viz in this County.

The Court proceeded to lay the County levy as follows towit:

```
The County is made                                          Dn
To William Irvine Clerk his salary for the year 1789 .....  1500
To John Snoddy Esqr Sheriff his ditto for ditto ..........  1500
To Thomas Hall States Attorney his ditto for ditto .......  1500
To Clerk his allowance under the Tax Law ..............     1000
To the Clerk for to purchase books ....................     1780
To the Clerk for attending a call court ..................   200
To the Sheriff for ditto ...............................     200
                                                            7080
To deposition ............................... 1700[4700]
Credit by 1179 tiths at 10 pounds each .......... 1179[11790]
```

Order that Thomas **Kennedy**, George **Adams**, James **Henderson** and Richard **Rannells** [*Bramwell*] or any three appraise Denis **Devers** estate and report.

Commonwealth vs Robert [*John*] **Mathews** fine suspended until further order of this Court and the sheriff to release him out of custody.

Administrator of the estate of John **Colefoot** granted to Wallis **Estill**. Oath taken and bond security given. *Security is John Woods.*

Ordered that Archibald **Woods**, Sam **Estill**, John **Gass**, John **Mitchell** appraise John **Colefoot's** estate.

Ordered that Court Adjourn untill Court in Course.

George **Adams**

At a Court held for Madison County on Tuesday the first day of December 1789.

Present George **Adams**, James **Barnett**, Archibald **Woods** and Joseph **Kennedy**, gent.

A deed from James **Mason** and *Elizabeth his wife* to David **Maxwell** was acknowledged and Ordered recorded. fem relinquished.

Order that a stocks pillery and whiping poste be built and that John **Snoddy** present Sheriff be authorized to lett *the building of* the same to the lowest bidder.

An inventory and appraisment of the estate of Christopher **Irvine** Deceased was returned and Ordered recorded.

A deed from William **Robertson** and *Sarah his wife* to John **Pitman** *and Dorothy* **Peyton** *his wife*. Fem relinquished and Ordered recorded.

The alotment of Elizabeth **Turpins** right of dower returned and Ordered recorded.

On motion and oath of Charles **Campbell** a dedimus is granted him to take the deposition of Ame **Hiatt** vs *Humphrey* **Best**.

On the motion of William **Irvine** and Haile **Talbot** they are appointed guardians to Francis **Irvine** and Molly **Irvine** and David **Irvine**, orphans of Christopher **Irvine**, Deceased whereupon they entered into bond conditioned as the Law directs. *Securities are John* **Pitman**, *James* **French** *and Archibald* **Woods**.

The Sheriff returns a list or pole of an election for a Trustee for the Town of Boonsborough which is Ordered recorded.

A deed and Comm. from John **McKinsy** and *Nancy his wife* to John **Boyles** was acknowledged and Ordered recorded.

A deed from Samuel **Davis** to Samuel **Boyd** and *Jane his wife* was proved by the oaths of John **Black**, Samuel **Black** and Benjamin **Duncan** and Ordered recorded.

The road from *William* **Ham's** Mill to intersect the Tates Creek Road is discontinued and no longer considered a public road.

Order that Court be adjourned until Court in Course.

Madison County, Kentucky Court Order Book A   79

George **Adams**

At a Court *of Quarter Session* held for Madison County the 2nd day of February 1790.

Present George **Adams**, David **Gass**, Archibald **Woods**, Aaron **Lewis** and Robert **Rodes**, gent.

A power of attorney from Green **Clay** to William **Irvine** was proved by the oath of Peter **Woods** and Ordered recorded.

Present James **Barnett** and Moses **Dooley**, gent.

Andrew **Kennedy**, foreman; Stephen **Handcock**, Edward **Williams**, Samuel **Freeman**, Peter **Taylor**, Richard **Gentry**, Zach **Dozier**, William **Pollard**, William **Dunham**, Robert **Kilpatrick**, Leonard **Hetherly**, Samuel **Boyd**, Alex **Reed**, Samuel **Woods**, John **Maxwell**, Lofty **Pullins**, were sworn as a Grand Jury for this County having received their charge retired to consider of their presentments.

Charles **Dibriel**, gent. present.

On the motion of Fothergil **Adams** a license is granted him to celebrate the rights of marriage whereupon he took the oath of fidelity. *Produced credentials from the Baptist Church.*

William **Jones** an inspector of **Collier's** and **Boone's** whearehouses took the oath required by Law whereupon he entered into bond conditioned at the Law directs.

Joseph **Brown** appeared in discharge of his recognizance and on motion of Richard **Rannalls** it is ordered that the said Joseph **Brown** be bound to his good behavior to all the liege people of this Commonwealth and in particular to the said Richard **Rannells**. Joseph **Brown**, John **Brown** and Thomas **Wilmore** [*Wilburn*] came into Court and acknowledged themselves severally bound unto his Excellency the Governor in the sums following to wit: The said Joseph in the sum of one hundred pounds and the said John and Thomas in the sum of £ 50 each. To be void upon the following conditions to wit. That the said Joseph peacefully behave himself for the term of a year and a day from the present date to all the liege people of this Commonwealth and in particular to Richard **Rannells**.

Madison County, Kentucky Court Order Book A

The Grand Jury returned into Court and presented Joseph **Merritt**, Elisha **Brooks**, Jacob **Burgin**, Joseph **Brown** and Thomas **Fugit** and it is ordered that the Clerk issue summons against the persons presented.

James **Barnett** vs *Thomas* **Kennedy** continued defendant.

Thomas **Kennedy** vs *James* **Barnett** continued plaintiff. *In Trespass, Assault and Battery.*

James **Barnett** vs *Thomas* **Kennedy** (in slander) continued. *In Trespass, Assault and Battery.*

William **Bush** vs *John* **Holly** continued. *In Trespass.*

Frederick **Repardon** vs *William* **Simpson** continued.

John **Holder** vs *William* **Hoy** continued.

Abraham **Burton** vs *William* **Orchard** continued.

Simon **Gentry** vs *Jeremiah* **Parker** Jury to enquire and John **Mitchell**, James **Harris**, Moses **Faris**, Thomas **Faris**, John **Pitman**, Joseph **Titus**, Henry **Bowyer**, John **Brown**, John **Anderson**, Andrew **Harris**, John **Black** and Nicholas **Hawkins** returned a verdict for £ 22-15-11 damages and costs.

Ordered that James **Barnett** pay Jesse **Noland**, Asa **Searcy**, Benjamin **Cooper** for one days attendance each against *Thomas* **Kennedy**.

John **Pitman** commissioner of the tax in the room of Hale **Talbot**.

William **Bush** vs *John* **Holly** dedimus to take deposition of Edward **Ahern** a witness in behalf of defendants.

William **Harrison** vs *Zachariah* **Dozier**. Thomas **Sutherland** special bail.

Ordered that the *scales* and weights furnished by Aaron **Lewis** and Robert **Rodes**, gent. at **Collier's** warehouse be renewed by the inspector and hereafter used there.

Hezekiah **Compton** [*Crumpton*] vs *Aaron* **King**. Samuel **Coughran** special bail, former bail released.

Ordered that Robert **Rodes**, Haile **Talbot**, John **Collier** and Aaron **Lewis** or any three do review the road from top of the hill to John **Collier's** warehouse.

Samuel **Hopper** vs *Samuel* **Bickerstaff** continued.

John **Phelps** vs *Robert* **Burton** refered to Charles **Dibrell** and John **Goggins** and their empire.

Same vs Same.

Same vs Same.

Robert **Burton** to pay William **Harvey** 1 days attendance vs **Phelps**.
Harry **Innis** assee vs *George* **Teter**. Thomas **Gest** special bail and judgment confessed per specialty. *£ 12 and costs.*
Ordered that the Court adjourn until 9 oclock tomorrow.

George Adams

Wednesday the third day of February 1790.
Present George **Adams**, Archibald **Woods**, John **Miller** and Robert **Rodes**, gent.

James **McNitt** surveyor of the road in room of Joseph **Scott**. George **Adams**, gent. to allott the tithes.
Report on road from John **Collier's** to the warehouse returned and Ordered recorded and voted established. John **Wilson** to clear the same.
Ordered that William **Miller**, Isaac **Anderson**, Michael **Faris** and William **Moore** Jr. or any three view a way for a road from Paint Lick to John **Cochran's** Mill and report.
Samuel **Brown** vs *Elisha* **Brooks** judgment for £ 2-15 and costs.
On motion of Barney **Stagner** by his attorney an injunction is granted him to stay proceedings upon a judgment obtained against him in this Court by the Trustees of Harrodsburg. Bill filed, oaths made, bond to be given in the ofice in twenty days with Thomas **Baker** his security.
William **McCullough** vs *Thomas* **White** continued.
James **McConnell's** administrator vs *David* **Noble** judgment *awarded plaintiff* and note *£ 2-4* with interest *from 12 June 1787.*
John **Courtney** vs *Israel* **Harmon** judgment for costs.
John **Courtney** to pay Thomas **Kennedy** 2 days attendance against **Harmon**.
Thomas **Southerland** vs *Nicholas* **Proctor** discontinued agreed.
John **Barnett** vs *Andrew* **Donalson** continued. *In trespass, assault and battery.*
Robert **Todd** *assee* vs *David* **Noble** continued.
Benjamin **Northcutt** by *George Adams* vs *Luke* **Moore**. Jury to try issue towit. William **Robertson**, William **Shinall**, John **McLean**, Joseph **Titus**, Aquilla **White**, Thomas **Baker**, Alex **Reed**, Sarshwile **Cooper**, Edward

Williams, James **Harris**, William **Holland** and Page **Portwood** returned verdict for £ 4-3 and new trial for plaintiff *on his paying costs.*
Present Joseph **Kennedy** and James **Barnett**, gent.
John **White** vs *Robert* **Tevis** judgment confessed for costs.
James **Hogan** asee vs *William* **Hoy** continued.
Commonwealth vs *Samuel* **Rice** continued.
Same vs *John* **Helton** continued.
Same vs *James* **Martin** continued.
Same vs *William* **Morison** judgment for costs.
Same vs *Thomas* **Baker** dismissed.
Azariah **Martin** vs *John* **Bruse**. Thomas **Kennedy** special bail.
On motion of William **Kerley** a didemus is granted him to take the depostion of Edward **Williams** against William **Sutherland.**
William **Southerland** vs *William* **Kerley** continued.
Hezekiah **Crampton** vs *Aaron* **King** continued for defendant.
William **Dryden** vs *Thomas* **Reynolds** judgment £ 2-8-0 *and costs.*
On the motion of Hesi **Crampton** a dedimus is granted him to take the deposition of James **Ross** vs **King.**
Charles **Campbell** vs *Humphrey* **Best** continued for plaintiff.
Richard **Hickman** *Lydia his wife* vs *Christopher* **Irvine** heirs on hearing the bill and answer. Ordered that James **French**, John **Miller**, Christopher **Greenup**, Thomas **Todd** and James **Brown** or any three do lay offto the complaintants the dower prayed for in the bill of complaint and make report thereof to this Court.
John **Jones** vs *William* **McCoullough** continued.
John **Miller** vs *John* **Adams** and *Jesse* **Noland** judgment £ 4-7 and costs.
Humphrey **Best** to Stephen **Best** 1 day. John **Weldon** same.
Joseph **Welden** same against **Campbell.**
John **McLean** vs *William* **Holland** continued.
Joseph **Kennedy**, Esqr produced a Commission appointing him Major whereupon he took the oath acquired by Law.
John **Warren** vs *Hugh* **Ross** continued.
Ordered that Harris **Massey** and David **Lynch** be summoned to show why the Courthouse is not completed.
Joseph **Proctor** vs *Hugh* **Ross** judgment for £ 3 *and costs.*
Jesse **Noland** vs *George* **Redman** continued.
Samuel **Brown** vs *Elisha* **Brooks** continued.

John **Crow** vs *Squire* **Boon** continued.
William **Perrel** vs *Jeremiah* **Parker** and *Thomas* **Farris**.
Order that the Court adjourn until Court in Course.

James **Barnett**

At a Court held for Madison County on Tuesday the second day of March 1790.
Present David **Gass**, James **Barnett**, John **Boyles**, Archibald **Woods**, Joseph **Kennedy** and Moses **Dooley**, gent.

A deed from Joseph **Craig** to William **Miller** was proved by the oaths of William **Clark** and James **Clark** also that *they saw* Margaret **Clark**, deceased signed the same as a witness which is Ordered recorded.

A deed from Green **Clay** to David **Hall** was proved by the oath of Edward **Parker** and John **Adams** and ordered to be certified.

A deed from Green **Clay** to John **Clark** was proved by oath of Godfrey **Clark** and David **Hall** and ordered to be certified.

A bond from Robert and Thomas **Lackey** to Robert **Henry** was proved by the oath of William **Barnett** and Jacob **Patton** and ordered to be recorded.

Same to the Same proved by the Same witnesses and ordered to be recorded.

On the Petition of John **Kennedy** seting forth that there is a mistake in the bounds of his tract of land known by the name of the Locust Bent Settlement and preemption. Order that the surveyor resurvey the tract and report.

Ordered that John **Leverage** be appointed surveyor of the road in the room of John **Pitman**.

On motion of Ellender **Black** and John **Black** letters of administration is granted them on the estate of James **Black**, deceased whereupon they entered into bond conditioned as the Law directs and took the oath required by Law. *Securities are John* **Boyles** *and David* **Gass**.

Ordered that George **Adams**, John **Miller**, James **Barnett** and Samuel **Boyd** be appointed to appraise the estate of James **Black** deceased.

Present John **Miller**, gent.

On motion of Joseph **Scott** by his attorney an injunction is granted him against Thomas **Bowyer** to stay all proceedings upon the judgment replevy bond. **Bowyer** vs **Scott**, bill filed, oath made, bonds and security given.

On the motion of Cornelius **Maupin** his ear mark a crop and slit in the right and a hole in the left Ordered recorded.

Margaret **Burnett** her ear mark a crop and slit in the right and hole and under keel in the left is Ordered recorded.

Margaret **Burnett** widow and relict of Rowland **Burnett** relinquished all benefit or advantage which she might claim under the will of the said Rowland her late husband which is ordered *to be certified*.

Rowland **Burnetts** will proved by William **Wallace** and William **Chenall** and Ordered recorded and John **Miller** and Cornelius **Maupin** two of the executors therein named obtained a certificate for probate thereof. Oath made and bond and security given. *Secutrities are William **Chenault** and William **Irvine**.*

Ordered that Thomas **Shelton**, Archibald **Woods**, John **Bratton** and William **Carr** appraise the estate of Roland **Burnett**, deceased.

Ordered that John **Sapington**, Peter **Evans**, Benjamin **Persley** [*Pursel*] and William **Calk** be appointed to view the way for a road from opposite **to Holder's** boatyard to intersect the road from Boonsborough to Madison Courthouse.

Ordered that Joseph **Kennedy**, gent. lott the tithes to work under the Nicholas **Hawkins**.

Ordered that George **Adams**, gent. former sheriff be summon to appear at the next Court to shew cause why he has not paid up the arrarages of the levy for 1787.

Ordered that it be certified to his Excellency the Governor that the Commission of David **Gass**, gent. as Sheriff of this County has not come to hand and that this Court has reason to believe that it is lost.

William **McCullough** vs *Thomas* **White** dismissed at the defendant costs.

Absent Joseph **Kennedy**, gent.

John **Jones** vs *William* **McColough** dismissed defendants costs.

Thomas **Hall**, William **Irvin**, James **Barnett**, Thomas **Maxwell** and John **Pitman** acknowledged themselves severally bound to the worshipful court of Madison County in the sum of two hundred pounds to be paid to the said Court and their successors. To be void on the following conditions that

Thomas **Lewis** behave and demean himself well to all the good people of this Commonwealth and that in case the said Thomas should hereafter be proved a slave that the said cognizors be bound to deliver the said Thomas to his master when applied for.

Ordered that Peter **Evans** be appointed surveyor in the room of Thomas **Stevens**.

On motion of John **Snoddy**, gent. Alex **Boyles** is admitted to qualify as his deputy.

Ordered that Court do adjourn until Court in Course.

David **Gass**

At a Court held for Madison County Tuesday the 6th day of April 1790.

Present George **Adams**, James **Barnett**, Joseph **Kennedy** and Aaron **Lewis**, gent.

Ordered that the Court adjourn till tomorrow 10 o'clock.

George **Adams**

At a Court continued and held on Wednesday the 7th day of April.

Present George **Adams**, Archibald **Woods**, Aaron **Lewis**, Robert **Rodes** and John **Holly**, gent. Absent George **Adams**. Present David **Gass**, gent.

Order that John **Kincade**, Jr., Samuel **Coughran**, Matthew **Scott** and James **Robinson** [*Robertson*] or any three do view the nearest and most convenient way from Paint Lick to John **Coughran's** Mill and from thence to John **Kincade's**, Jr. and make report thereof.

William **Hoy's** last will and testament was proved by the oaths of William **Jones**, William **Holland** and John **Rush** witnesses thereto and ordered to record.

George **Adams**, gent. former sheriff of this county appeared agreeable to a summons of the last court and for reasons appearing to the Court same is ordered to be continued untill the next Court.

Administration on the Estate of John **Blockley**, deceased was granted to Benjamin **Okley** who executed and acknowledged bond in the Sum of thirty pounds with Harris **Massey** and Samuel **Bickerstaffe** his securities conditioned as the Law directs.

William **Hancock** vs *John* **Broughton** [*Bratton*] dismissed at Defendant costs.

The certificate of John **Pitmans** having taken the oath of Commissioner of the Tax in this County was returned and ordered to be recorded.

Charles **Campbell** vs. *Humphrey* **Best** continued.
John **McClane** vs *William* **Holland** continued.
John **Warren** vs *Hugh* **Ross** continued.
Jesse **Noland** vs *George* **Redman** continued.
John **Crow** vs *Squire* **Boone** continued.
Samuel **Brown** vs *Elisha* **Brooks** continued.
William **Terrill** vs *Parker* and *Farris* continued.
Andrew **Hare** vs **Jones** and **Hickman** als.
John **Reed** vs *William* **McClure** continued.
Andrew **Hare** vs *John* **Woods**, etc. continued.
Same vs *William* **Hoy** abates defendants death.
Same vs Same Same.
Harry **Innes** vs *Michael* **McNeely** continued.
James **McManas** vs *Daniel* **Hicks** continued.
Andrew **Hare** vs *Isaiah* **Jackson** Als Sums.
William **Holland** vs *Thomas* **Roberts** continued.
Samuel **Irvin** vs *Moses* **Riddle** continued.

Ordered that Court be adjourned untill Court in Course.

David **Gass**

At a Court of Quarter Sessions held at Madison County on Tuesday the 4th day of May 1790.

Present George **Adams**, James **Barnett**, Archibald **Woods**, Joseph **Kennedy** and Moses **Dooley**.

Moses **Dooly** vs *George* **Teter** dismissed at defendants costs.

James **Allen**, Esqr for reason appearing to the Court is admitted to Qualify as an attorney at Law.

Samuel **Woods**, foreman; Andrew **Kennedy**, Henry **Owley**, Zachariah **Dozier**, John **Maxwell**, John **Davis**, Joseph **Weldon**, Lofty **Pollins**, Joseph **Scott**, Edward **Turner**, John **Sappington**, Isaac **Williams**, William **Brisco**, Benjamin **Oakley**, Robert **Kilpatrick** and John **Kincaid** was sworn a Grand

Jury for this County having received their charge retired to consider of there presentments.

Reuben **Stivers** vs *Jacob* **Burgen** discontinued.

Hezekiah **Crampton** vs *Aaron* **King** dismissed at plaintiff costs except the defendants attorney fee.

A deed from William **Hoy** to Zach **Dozier** was fully proved by the oath of Richard **Tunstall** ordered Recorded.

William **Parrel** [***Purnel***] vs *Parker* and **Farris** dismissed.

Robert **Todd** assee vs *David* **Noble** discontinued agreed.

The grand jury returned into Court and made the following presentments Peter **Taylor** for swearing three profane oaths by information of George **Adams**.

Peter **Taylor** for getting drunk by information of George **Adams**.

The surveyors of the road from Taylor's Fork to **Wood's** Station by the knowledge of our own body and having nothing farther to present were discharged.

Ordered that Isaac **Mise**, Joel **Hill**, Wilis **Cook** and John **Clark** or any three of them do appraise the estate of John **Blockley**, deceased.

A deed and Commission from James **Adams** and *Aggnes his wife* to Joseph **Weldon** before acknowledged and ordered to be recorded.

Ordered that George **Adams**, John **Bruce** and Samuel **Rice** do view the Courthouse as built by Harris **Massie** and David **Lynch** and report wether the same be performed agreeable to contract.

John **Bruce** vs *Azariah* **Martin** dedimus to take the deposition of Isham **Pruitt** and Jonathan **Longstreth**.

Azariah **Martin** vs *John* **Bruce** dedimus to take the deposition of Anthony **Pruitt** de benesse.

Samuel **Hopper** vs *Samuel* **Bigerstaff** continued.

Commonwealth vs Robert **Brooks** judgment for 5 *shillings* and costs. *Defendant did not appear so ruled for plaintiff.*

Same vs Elisha **Brooks** judgment same.

Same vs Jacob **Burgin** judgment for same.

Same vs Joseph **Brown** not guilty.

Same vs Joseph **Merit** judgment for 5 *shillings* and costs.

Same vs Thomas **Fuget** als.

Martin **Turpin** assee vs *John* **McMullin** judgment for costs.

James **Barnett** vs *Thomas* **Kennedy** jury sworn to try issue towit. John **Carpenter**, William **Robinson**, Barney **Stagner**, James **Anderson**, William **Kerley**, James **Howard**, Thomas **Baker**, Thomas **Gist**, Samuel **Boyd**, Sherwood **Harris**, Haile **Talbot** and Stephen **Hancock** returned verdict for plaintiff for £ 2-5 damages and Judgment.

Thomas **Southerland** vs *John and James* **McQueens** dismissed at defendant costs.

John **Reid** vs *William* **McClure** continued for defendant.

Benjamin **Northcut** *by his next friend George* **Adams** vs *Luke* **Moore** continued.

On the motion of Benjamin **Cooper** his ear mark a hole in each ear Ordered recorded.

On motion of Samuel **Brown** his ear mark a crop and over keel in right ear and over keel in the left ear Ordered recorded.

William **Galispie** vs *Jeremiah* **Perry** dedimus to take the deposition of Jacob **Lewis** and John **Holeman**.

Edward **Williams** vs *Thomas* **Guist** motion continued untill tomorrow.

Ordered that the Court adjourn untill tomorrow 10 o'clock.

George **Adams**

At a Court continued and held for Madison County on Wednesday 5th day of May 1794 (sic).

Present Archibald **Woods**, Joseph **Kennedy**, Robert **Rodes** and John **Miller**, gent.

Ordered that John **Collier** be appointed to build a wearhouse 24 feet by 40 and a house for the scales and weights 24 feet by 18 feet and that Aaron **Lewis** and Robert **Rodes** be appointed as Commissioners to superintend the buildings.

Present George **Adams**, gent.

Allen **Burton** vs *Charles* **Dibrell** dismissed.

An instrument of writing from Samuel **Campbell** to Thomas **Kennedy** was proved by oath of Green **Clay** and Ordered recorded.

Thomas **Gest** vs *Edward* **Williams** injunction disolved and bill dismissed at complaintants costs.

A resurvey of John **Kennedy's** preemptions was returned Ordered Certified.

James **Barnett** vs Thomas **Kennedy** jury to try issue viz. Thomas **Gist**, Andrew **Harris**, John **Manier**, James **McCollester**, James **Hendricks**, James **White**, William **Brown**, James **Burnsides**, Samuel **Woods**, Thomas **Shelton**, Robert **Moore** and Thomas **Batts** and returned verdict for plaintif £ 2-5. Motion for new trial rejected. *The defendant did speak the slanderous words in the declaration mentioned.*

James **Hogen** assee vs William **Hoy** continued.

Andrew **Hare** vs William **Harris** order of reference *to arbitration* set aside and continued.

Thomas **Kennedy** vs James **Barnett** dismissed. *Plaintiff to pay costs.*

William **Bush** vs John **Holly** continued with costs.

John **Holder** vs William **Hoy** continued.

Commonwealth vs John **Helton** dismissed.

Same vs Samuel **Rice** dismissed.

Same vs James **Martin** continued.

John **Barnett** vs Andrew **Donelson** continued.

Thomas **Kennedy** vs James **Barnett** to pay Alexander **Reed** one day. Present Charles **Debrell**, gent.

James **Barnett** to pay Sarshwill **Cooper** one day vs Thomas **Kennedy**.

Ordered that the surveyor of this County have leave of absence from his County until the first of October next.

On motion of Sarshwill **Cooper** his ear mark a crop in the left and under keel in the right is Ordered recorded.

Barnett to pay David **Lynch** two days attendance vs **Kennedy**.

John **Bruce** special bail for Jonathan **Longstreth** against **Gordon** and **Coburn** delivered up the body of the said Jonathan in discharge of his recognizance. Whereupon the said Jonathan **Longstreth** was prayed and ordered in custody.

James **Barnett** to pay Asa **Searcy** for three days attendance vs **Kennedy** 1 day in slander.

Abraham **Burton** vs William **Orchard** continued.

James **Barnett** to pay Humphrey **Best** for 2 days attendance against **Kennedy** in the assault and battery.

William **Sutherland** vs *William* **Kerley** jury to try issue viz. Alex **Reid**, Harris **Massie**, John **Persons**, William **Hamm**, John **Pitman**, John **Weldon**, John **Hopkins**, Joseph **Weldon**, James **Robinson** [*Robertson*], Nicholas **Hawkins**, William **Small** and Anthony **Rogers**. Plaintiff failing to prosecute is non such.

Andrew **Hare** vs **Woods** and **Spring** dismissed agreed.

Charles **Dibrell** vs *Isaac* **Burton** dismissed at defendants costs.

George **Boyd** vs *Thomas* **Batts** continued at defendants costs.

Lucy **Searcy** vs *Thomas* **Robards** continued for garnishee to declare what property he hath in his hands.

The persons appointed to view the Courthouse reported that it is built agreeable to contract and this Court doth receive the same and that the undertakers bond be given up to them.

William **Woods** vs *Thomas* **Chinn** dismissed [*continued*].

James **Lowry** vs *John* **Armstrong** same.

George **Boyd** to pay Hardy **Rolls** two days attendance and traveling 18 miles against *Thomas* **Batts**.

Same to pay **Jonathan Owsley** two days attendance.

Frederick **Raperdan** vs *William* **Simson** continued.

William **Harrison** vs *Zachariah* **Dozier** continued.

Joseph **Weldon** vs *James* **Robinson** [*Robertson*] refered to Thomas **Kennedy** and George **Adams**.

Thomas **Kennedy** vs *Robert* **Dean** continued.

John **Welden** and ux vs *Robert* **Adams** same.

William **Caldwell** vs *James* **Matthews** continued.

Patrick **Galliher** vs *John* **Martin** continued. *In trespass, assault and battery.*

Robert **Adams** vs *Joseph* **Weldon** and ux continued.

Azariah **Martin** vs *John* **Bruce** continued.

John **Dozier** vs *Matthew* **Walker** continued.

Court adjourned till Court in Course.

George **Adams**

At a Court held for Madison County on Tuesday the first day of June 1790.

Present George **Adams**, James **Barnett**, John **Boyles**, Archibald **Woods**, Joseph **Kennedy**, Robert **Rodes**, John **Miller** and John **Hally**.

Commonwealth vs William **Ham** collection of the fine suspended until further order.

Ordered that David **Kincaid**, Samuel **Jamison**, John **Campbell**, Will **Butcher** or any three of them do view the nearest or best way for a road from Madison Courthouse to John **Kinkead's**, Jr. and make report thereof.

A deed from Stephen **Merritt** to Michael **Wallace** was acknowledged and ordered to be recorded.

A deed of Commission from Benjamin **Quinn** *and Franky his wife* to John **Mobley** was proved by the oath of Edward **Mobley**, William **Addison** and Benjamin **Mobley** and Ordered recorded.

A power of attorney from Joseph **McQueen** and *Margaret his wife* to Richard **Ellson** was acknowledged and Ordered recorded.

Ordered that David **Gass** and James **Barnett**, gent. be recommended to his Excellency the Governor as proper persons to act as Sheriff. Also that the Clerk do inform his Excellency the Governor the circumstance of the Commission coming too late to hand.

A deed from John **Morton** and *Sarah his wife* to James **Hendricks** was acknowledged and Ordered recorded. femme relinquished.

Alexander **Reed** vs *Robert* **Deane** dismissed.

A deed from George **Boone** and *Ann his wife* to James **Hendricks** was acknowledged and Ordered recorded. femme relinquished.

A deed from the Same to Matthew **Fowler** was acknowledged and Ordered recorded. femme relinquished.

A resurvey of John **Kennedy's** preemption was returned and ordered to be certified.

Ordered that Closs **Thompson** be exempted from paying County Levy.

Ordered that John **Watson** be exempted from paying County Levy.

A deed from Benjamin **Quinn** and *Franky his wife* to Thomas **Jones** was proved by oath of John and Edward **Mobley** and William **Addison** ordered to be recorded.

A deed from Higerson **Grubbs** and *Lucy his wife* to James **Johnson** was acknowledged and Ordered recorded. femme relinquished.

A deed from same to William **Pollard** femme relinquished being before acknowledged and Ordered recorded.

Same to Isaac **Williams** same order.

Same to William **Williams** same order.

An inventory and apraisment of the estate of James **Blockley** [*Black*], deceased was returned and Ordered recorded.

A deed from Michael **McNeely** to John **Leverage** is acknowledged and Ordered recorded.

Same to Same Same order.

Ordered that Green **Clay**, Jacob **Starns**, John **South** and Peter **Evans** do view a way for a road from the mouth of Jacks Creek to Col. *Aaron* **Lewis's** Mill.

Ordered that the road from William **Irvines** to where it intersects the road that leads from **Woodses** Station is established and that Richard **Callaway** be appointed surveyor of the same and Archibald **Woods** gent do lott of the tithes to work under him.

A deed from Joseph **Scott** to Mathew **Scott** was acknowledged and Ordered recorded.

Abraham **Burton** vs *William* **Orchard** dismissed agreed.

Present Aaron **Lewis** and Charles **Debriell** gent.

A deed from John **South** to Page **Portwood** was acknowledged and Ordered recorded.

Ordered that a ferry be established from the mouth of Tates Creek to the opposite shore across the Kentucky on the name of David **Wilcocks** and Jesse **Cofer** and that they give bond in the Clerk's office as the Law directs.

On the motion of William **Ham** his ear mark a crop of the right ear is Ordered recorded.

Ordered that Thomas **Batts** be appointed surveyor of the road in room of Samuel **Teter** and that Moses **Dooley**, gent. lott the tithes.

Ordered that Volent **Stone**, Joshua **Stamper**, John **Wilkerson** and Benjamin **Pursley** do view a way for a road from the mouth of Callaway Creek to Joshua **Stamper** and make report.

Ordered that Francis **Holly**, John **Carpenter**, Jacob **Miller** and Archibald **Woods** view the road from the broad ford of Otter Creek to James **Walkers** and make report.

John **Phelps** vs *Robert* **Barton** order reference *to arbitration* set aside and continued.

On the motion of James **French** this Court relinquishes all right to a slip of the publick land that was extended to include a spring to the Trustees of the Town of Milford to be by them disposed off as the Law directs.

Ordered that the Court adjourn till Court in Course.

George **Adams**

At a Court held fof Madison County on Tuesday the 6th day of July 1790.

Present George **Adams**, David **Gass**, John **Boyles**, Archibald **Woods** and Robert **Rodes**, gent.

A deed from Abraham **Buford** to *Edward* **Taylor** was proved by the oath of William **Ham**, Allen **Burton** and Thomas **Gulley** and Ordered recorded.

A deed from same to George **Hinton** was proved by the oath of Edward **Taylor**, William **Ham** and Allen **Burton** and Ordered recorded.

A deed from George **Smith** by his attorney in fact to Andrew **Huston** was proved by the oath of Jesse **Huston**, Samuel **Morrow** and John **Knox** & Ordered recorded.

A deed from Green **Clay** to John **Clark** was proved fully by the oath of William **Jones** and Ordered recorded.

Ordered that Benjamin **Wheler** be appointed Constable in the room of William **Holland**.

Ordered that John **Reid** be appointed surveyor of the road in room of Alexander **Reid**.

A deed from William **Patton** to James **McNutt** was proven by the oath of James **Barnett**, Joseph **Barnett** and Francis **McNutt** and Ordered recorded.

The report of an *alteration* of a road from the broad ford of Otter Creek to James **Walkers** was returned and Ordered recorded and the surveyor is order to cut it accordingly.

Page **Portwood** vs *Thomas* **Southerland** dismissed.

A deed from William **Pollard** and *Anne his wife* to William **Bridges** was acknowledged and Ordered recorded. femme relinquished.

Ordered that James **McCalisters** and Andrew **Miller** be recommended as Captain in the Militia and Robert **Kincaid** as Lieutenant also David **Kennedy** and Robert **Knox** as Ensigns in the Militia.

Return of a election of Trustees for the Town of Boonesboro is Ordered recorded.

Roland **Hoy**, John **South**, Richard **Tunsdale** executors named in the last will and testament of William **Hoy** deceased obtained probate and certified. Whereupon they took the oath required by law and entered into bond with James **Barnett**, George **Adams**, Adam **Woods**, John **Miller**, William **Miller** and William **Jones** there security conditioned as the Law directs.

Ordered that Robert **Woods**, Aaron **Lewis**, David **Crews** and William **Irvine** be appointed to appraise the estate of William **Hoy** Deceased.

Ordered that Archibald **Woods**, gent. be added to the order for Aaron **Lewis** and Robert **Rodes**, gent. viewing a convenient place for a whearhouse at Boonsborough.

Jane **Burton** appeared in discharge of her recognizance and on the motion of Elizabeth **Willis** it is ordered that the said Jane **Burton** be bound to her good behavior to all the lige people of this Commonwealth and in particular to the said Elizabeth **Willis**. Jane **Burton**, William **West** and Thomas **Brockman** came into Court and acknowledged themselves severally bound unto his Excellency the Governor in the sums following to wit. The said Jane in the sum of fifty pounds and the said William and Thomas in the sum of £5 each to be void on the following conditions towit that the said Jane peaceably behave herself for the term of one year and a day to all the lige people of this Commonwealth and in particular to Elizabeth **Willis**.

Ordered that James **Barnett**, George **Adams**, William **Miller** and Robert **Henderson** review the way for a road from about half a mile south of the crossing of the road from Michael **Henderson** to the meeting house at a branch to the junction of the new and old road.

On motion of Samuel **Cochran** his ear mark a crop of the right and under keel in the left is Ordered recorded.

A report of a road from the mouth of Callaway's Creek to Joshua **Stamper's** was returned and Ordered recorded. Ordered that Volintine **Stone** be appointed surveyor of the above road and Aaron **Lewis**, gent. to allott the tiths to work on the same.

Ordered that Jacob **Dooley**, David **England**, Christopher **Horn**, Reubin **Gentry** be appointed to view the way from *Aaron* **Lewis** Mill through **Hodge's** settlement to Boonsborough.

A deed from Higgason **Grubbs** to John **Embry** was acknowledged and Ordered recorded.

A deed from same to Benjamin **Morton** was acknowledged and Ordered recorded.

A deed from Higerson **Grubbs** to Robert **Rodes** acknowledged and ordered recorded.

A deed from same to John **Moore** acknowledged and ordered recorded.

A deed from same to Joel **Embry** acknowledged and ordered recorded.

Ordered that Adam **Woods**, Nathan **Hawkins** and William **Craft** *[Crath]* to view and value the stocks and whipping post and make report to next Court.

Jane **Burton**, Senr. in discharge of her recognizance and on the motion of Elizabeth **Willis** is ordered that the said Jane **Burton** be bound to her good behavior whereupon Jane **Burton**, Allen **Burton**, Thomas **Gully** came into Court and acknowledge themselves severally bound to his Excellency the sum of £ 100 the said Jane and Allen and Thomas in the sum of £ 50 each to be void on the following conditions that the said Jane be of good behavior for the term of one year and a day to all the Commonwealth lege people and particularly to the said Elizabeth **Willis**.

Ordered that the Court be adjourned until Court in course.

George **Adams**

At a Court called and held at Madison Courthouse on Tuesday the 6th day of July 1790 for the examination of John **Anderson** charged with accidently kiling Jesse **Watson** before the worshipful Court of George **Adams**, David **Gass**, James **Barnett**, John **Boyles**, Aaron **Lewis**, Robert **Rodes**, John **Miller**, John **Halley** and Charles **Debriell**, gent. The prisoner being led to the barr and being demanded whether he was guilty of the charge aforesaid says it was an accident whereupon sundry witnesses being examined on behalf of the Commonwealth and the prisoner heard in his own defense on consideration of the matter whereof it is the *unanimous* opinion of the Court that the said John **Anderson** is not guilty and that he be discharged by the unanimous opinion of the Court and the Court then dissolved.

George **Adams**

At a Court begun and held at Madison Courthouse on Tuesday the 3rd day of August 1790.

Present George **Adams**, John **Boyles**, Archibald **Woods**, Joseph **Kennedy** and Robert **Rodes**, gent.

The deposition of Nathan **Hawkins** is acknowledged and Ordered recorded.

Thomas **Kennedy**, foreman; Stephen **Handcock**, David **Wells**, Samuel **Freeman**, Hugh **Campbell**, John **White**, Joseph **Scott**, John **Sappington**, Andrew **Kennidy**, Jeremiah **Crews**, John **Kennidy**, Samuel [*John*] **Cochran**, John **Kincaid**, Zach **Dozier**, Joseph **Phelps**, Higgson **Grubbs** and Edward **Williams** and John **Brown** a Grand Jury was sworn for this County having received their charge retired to consider the presents.

A power of attorney from William **Hix** to James **Bogs** was proved by the oaths of William **Blithe** and John **Hunt** two of the witnesses thereto subscribed and ordered to be recorded.

Present John **Miller**, gent.

Ordered that Allen **Burton** be appointed Constable in the room of Benjamin **Wheeler**.

The noncupative will of Jesse **Watson** was proved the oaths of Evan and Thomas **Watson** and James **Stephenson** and Ordered recorded.

On the motion of James **Stephenson** and Milley **Watson** letters of administration with the will annexed on the estate of Jesse **Watson**, deceased whereupon they entered into bond conditioned as the law directs and took the oath required by law. *Securities are Evan Watson and Peter Taylor.*

Ordered that John **Pitman**, Thomas **Maxwell**, William **Morrison** and John **Devers** appraise the above estate.

The grand Jury returned and made the following presentments towit. James **Robinson**, Junr. for profain swearing. James **Robinson**, Senr. for the same. The surveyor of the road from Taylor Fork to *Archibald* **Woods** Station and the surveyor of the first part of the road from the mouth Tates Creek to Madison Courthouse and the above persons is ordered to be summoned.

Commonwealth vs *Joseph* **Brown** judgment for 5 shillings and costs.

Samuel **Hopper** vs *Samuel* **Bigerstaff** continued.

Samuel **Irwin** vs *Moses* **Riddel** judgment for 32/9 and costs. *£ 1-12-9.*

William **Bush** vs *John* **Halley** continued.

John **Phelps** vs *Robert* **Burton** discontinued.

Same vs Same same.

Rates of Liquor &c.
Rum at 12/.
Whiskey $1 per gallon.
Beer 2/ per gallon
Breakfast 1/
Dinner 1/3
Lodging six pence
Pasturage six pence
Corn four pence a pottle.

    Ordered that John **Hally**, gent. lott of the tithes to **Halley**.
    William **Harrison** vs *Zachariah* **Dozier** continued.
    Thomas **Kennedy** vs *Robert* **Dean** continued.
    John **Barnett** vs Andrew **Donelson** *continued, in trespass, assault and* battery.
    Benjamin **Northcut** *by George* **Adams** vs *Luke* **Moore** continued.
    Frederick **Raperdam** vs *William* **Simson** continued.
    John **Weldon** and ux vs *Robert* **Adams** continued.
    Robert Adams vs. **Weldon** *and wife continued.*
    Azariah **Martin** vs *John* **Bruce** continued.
    Francis **McNut** vs *Robert* **Deen** judgment *against debt* for £ 2.
    Ordered that Robert **Moore** make the necessary alteration in his road at the Buffalo Fork *a branch of Tates Creek.*
    John **Crow** vs *Squire* **Boon** dismissed.
    William **Gallispie** vs *Jeremiah* **Perry** dismissed each party to pay half the costs.
    The plan of the Town of Milford was returned and Ordered recorded.
    Patrick **Gallahar** vs *John* **Martin** continued, *in trespass, assault and* battery.
    Charles **Boyd** vs *Thomas* **Batts** continued.
    John **Phelps** vs *Robert* **Burton** acknowledgement filed and discontinued.
    John **Reid** vs *William* **McClure** continued for the defendant.
    Anthony **Rogers** vs *James* **Von** [*Vough*] continued.
    Allen **Burton** vs *Charles* **Debriell** continued.
    Patrick **Galliher** to pay James **Nevil** 1 day traveling 25 miles vs *John* **Martin**.

John **Crow** to pay *Josiah* **Boone** for 2 days vs *Squire* **Boon**.
John **Holder** vs *William* **Hoy** continued.
James **Hogen** assee *of John* **Colson** vs *William* **Hoy** continued.
Andrew **Hare** vs *William* **Harris** continued.
Jesse **Noland** vs *George* **Redmand** dismissed agreed.
Charles **Campbell** vs *Humphrey* **Best** for defendant.
John **Warren** vs *Hugh* **Ross** continued.
John **McLean** vs *William* **Holland** continued.
William **Holland** vs *Thomas* **Robards** continued.
Jonathan **Owsley** vs *James* **Shackelford** continued.
John **Fitzjareld** vs *Jeremiah* **Perry** continued.
Nathan **Huston** vs *Zachariah* **Dozier** continued.
Ordered that William **Kerley** be recommended as an Ensign in the Militia.
William **Hardage** vs *Thomas* **Sanders** dismissed for the want of bond.
Ordered that the Court adjourn until Court in Course.

George **Adams**

At a Court held for Madison County on Tuesday the 6th day of September 1790.

Present George **Adams**, Archibald **Woods**, Joseph **Kennedy**, Aaron **Lewis** and Moses **Dooley**, gent.

A power of attorney from Edmund **Hockaday** to John **Hockaday** was proved by the oath of William **Irvine** and Thomas **Reynolds** witnesses thereto subscribed and Ordered recorded.

A mortgage from Hick **Grubbs** to John **Tanner** was acknowledged and Ordered recorded.

Report of a road from the mouth of Jacks Creek to *Aaron* **Lewises** Mill was returned and Ordered recorded.

An inventory and appraisment of the estate of Rowland **Burnett** Deceased was returned and Ordered recorded.

A deed from Higgerson **Grubbs** to William **Noland** was acknowledged and Ordered recorded.

A deed from Robert **Henderson** and *Frances his wife* to Michael **Wallace** is acknowledged and ordered recorded. femme relinquished.

A deed from same to William **Mason** same order.

A deed from Whitson **George** and *Mary Ann his wife* to Robert **Henderson** was acknowledged and Ordered recorded. femme relinquished.

A deed from Robert **Henderson** and *Frances his wife* to William **Mason** acknowledged and ordered recorded. femme relinquished.

An appraisement of the estate of William **Hoy** deceased was returned and ordered recorded. Also an inventory of bond and accounts due said estate was returned and ordered recorded.

John **Sappington**, gent. produced a Commission from his Excellency the Governor appointing him Captain in the Militia whereupon he took the oath prescribed by Law.

A plot of land was laid off for **Colliers** warehouse was returned and ordered recorded.

A deed from Green **Clay** to James **Smith** was proved by the oath of Robert **Rodes**, David **Crews** and John **Collier** and ordered recorded.

Jonathan **Owsley** produced a Commission appointing him Captain whereupon he took the oaths prescribed by Law.

Ordered that Edward **Turner**, James **Martin**, John **Turner**, Robert **Rodes** or any three of them do view the hill at Jesse **Embry's** make report of the nearest and best way.

A deed and Commission from Robert **Henderson** and *Frances his wife* to Joseph **Horn** was returned and being before acknowledged.

Ordered that John **South** be appointed surveyor of the road from the mouth of Jacks Creek to Lewis Mill and have Aaron **Lewis**, gent. to a lott tithes to work on the same.

On the motion of Joseph **Titus** letters of administration is granted on the estate of Elizabeth **Stephenson** deceased whereupon he took the oath prescribed by Law and entered into bond. *Security is Boud Estill and John McClane.*

A deed from Cornelius **Daugherty** and *Margaret his wife* to Jesse **Embry** was acknowledged and ordered recorded. femme relinquished.

John **McClain** vs *William* **Holland** dismissed at defendant costs.

On the motion and oath of Thomas **Kennedy** a dedimus is granted him to take the deposition of John **Huston** vs *Robert* **Dean**.

Ordered that Adam **Woods**, Boud **Estill**, William **Maguire**, David **Wells** or any three of them being first sworn do appraise the estate of Elizabeth **Stephenson** deceased and make report thereof.

A deed from John **Holder** and *Frances his wife* to Mathew **Allegree** proved by the oath of John **Stepp**, William **Turpin** and Nathan **Turpin** and ordered recorded.

A deed from John **Holder** and *Frances his wife* to John **Stepp** was proven by the oath of William **Turpin**, Charles **Burrass** and Nathan **Turpin** and ordered recorded.

A deed from the same to William **Turpin** was proved by same witness.

Report of a road from Paint Lick to John **Kincaid**, Junr. was established and ordered recorded.

Also a report of a road from Madison Courthouse to John **Kincaid's**, Junr. was established and ordered recorded.

Ordered that Mathew **Scott** be appointed surveyor of the road from Paint Lick to the crossroads below Michael **Farris** and Samuel **Cochrans** from thence to John **Kincaid's**, Junr. and James **Barnett**, gent. to alot the tithes to work on the same. Also Samuel **Boyd** and John **Kincaid** surveyors of the road leading from Madison Courthouse to John **Kincaid's** and **Boyd** to begin at the Courthouse and go as far as a spring on the branch of Hart's Fork and John **Kincaid** from thence to John **Kincaid's**, Junr. and David **Gass**, gent. to allott the tithes to work on the same.

Order that Micaj **Faris** be appointed surveyor of the road in the room of James **Black**, deceased and David **Gass**, gent to alot the tithes to work on the same.

The inspectors of **Boon's** and **Collier's** warehouses returned the numbers of hogheads of tobacco inspected by them at the same and is ordered recorded.

Ordered that David **Crews**, John **Sappington**, James **Hendricks**, John **White** view a way for a road from **Woods** and **Carpenter's** Mill to intersect the Boonsborough Road where the Jacks Creek Road comes in and make report.

The persons appointed to appraise the stocks and whipping post made report which is ordered recorded.

Ordered that the sheriff summon Paton **Pryer** and Hornes **Nagle** to appear at the next Court.

Thomas **Parsley** vs *Leonard* **Dozier** als summons.

Madison County, Kentucky Court Order Book A   101

   John **Reed** vs *William* **McClure** judgment for £ 1-18-0.
   A list of surveys returned and ordered recorded.
   Ordered that Samuel **Given** as Lieutenant and John **Alcorn** and Stephen **Walker** be recommended as Ensigns.
   John **Warren** vs *Hugh* **Ross** *contnued.*
   Allen **Burton** vs *Charles* **Dibrell** continued.
   John **Tanner** vs *Higgason* **Grubbs** continued.
   John **Montgomery** vs *Robert* **Henderson** dismissed.
   Jonathan **Owsley** vs *James* **Shackelford** continued.
   Lucy **Searcy** vs *Thomas* **Roberds** continued.
   Same vs Same continued.
   John **Dozier** vs *Matthew* **Walker** continued.
   Anthony **Rogers** vs *James* **Von**[*Vaughn*] continued for defendant.
   John **South** vs *William and John* **Owsley** judgment confessed.
   The Reverend Charles **Kavanaugh** produced credentials of his being in regular communion with the Methodist Society whereupon he is licensed to celebrate the rights of marriages and he is to enter into bond in the Clerk's office whereupon he took the oath as required by Law.
   Ordered that Charles **Campbell** pay Robert **Burton** for six days attendance vs *Humphrey* **Best**.
   Ordered that Thomas **Montgomery**, James **French**, John **Goggins** be recommended as proper person to be added to the Commission of the Peace in this County.
   David **Gass**, James **Barnett**, Archibald **Woods**, Joseph **Kennedy**, Aaron **Lewis**, Robert **Rodes**, John **Miller** and John **Holly**, gent.
   Ordered that the Court adjourn till Court in Course.
              David **Gass**

At a Court held for Madison County at the Courthouse on Tuesday the 5th of October 1790.
   Present George **Adams**, David **Gass**, John **Boyle** and Robert **Rodes**, gent.

   A deed from Aaron **King** and *Hannah his wife* to John **Doty** and acknowledged and ordered recorded. femme relinquished.

A deed from Joseph **Bledsoe** to Joseph **Craig** was proved by John **Phelps**, Cary **Phelps** and Joseph **Baugh** and ordered recorded.

A deed from John **Sappington** and *Jemima his wife* to Hartley **Sappington** femme relinquished. and acknowledged and ordered recorded.

A deed from David **Cook** to James **Adams** was proved by John **Adams**, Richard **Walker** and Mathew **Adams** and ordered recorded.

A plan of the Town of Boonsborough was returned to the Court and ordered recorded.

Administration on the estate of Robert **Brank**, deceased granted to Robert **Brank** who executed and acknowledged bond in the penalty of £ 150 with Andrew **Kennedy** security bond conditioned as Law directs.

John **McCollister**, Captain; William **Anderson**, Lieutenant and Stephen **Walker**, Ensign severally took the oaths required by Law.

Barney **Stagner**, Ensign took the oaths required by Law.

George **Adams**, Thomas **Kennedy**, James **McHaney** and Alexander **Denny** or any three appointed to appraise the Estate of Robert **Brank**, deceased.

George **Adams**, Thomas **Kennedy**, James **McHaney** and Alexander **Denny** or any three of them to allot to Jane **Brank** widow of Robert **Brank**, deceased her dower out of the estate of the said decedent.

Ordered that George **Adams**, James **Barnett** and Robert **Henderson** and Andrew **Kennedy** view a way for a road from Thomas **Kennedy's** to Paint Lick and make report.

Ordered that Samuel **Estill** guardian of the orphans of James **Estill**, deceased be summon to appear.

Ordered that Richard **Gordon** be summoned to appear at the next Court.

The inventory and appraisement of the estate of Dennis **Dever** returned and ordered recorded.

Ordered that David **Crews**, John **South**, Thomas **Lawrence** and Alex **Davis** view a way for a road from David **Crews** to the Kentucky River between the mouths Ravin Creek and the old Fording.

Anthony **Rogers** vs *James* **Von**[*Vaughn*] judgment. £ 3-4.

A copy of a bond from James I. **Dozier** to Edward **Durbin** was proved by the oath of James **Sappington** and ordered recorded. Also the said Edward **Darbin** made oath of having lost the said original bond.

A deed from Reubin **Searcy** to Thomas **Parkham** proved by Asa **Searcy** and Stephen **Jett** and ordered recorded.

Lucy **Searcy** vs *Thomas* **Robards** attachment judgment. £ 7 and order sale. *Attached goods are 5 hogs, one hogshead of Tobacco and some corn.* Same vs Same attachment judgment. £ 3-9 and order sale.

Ordered new summons vs the garnisheer. *Green* **Clay** *and Cadd* **Jones** *summoned to appear as garnishees to declare what property they have of Thomas* **Robards**.

John **Dozier** vs *Matthew* **Walker** *Attached a gun.* judgment £ 15 and ordered sale.

John **Warren** vs *Hugh* **Ross** judgment for note and costs. £ *1-8.*

John **South** vs *Jonathan* **Owsley** *and James* **Shackelford** *writ of inquiry awarded to asses damages.* judgment awarded.

James **McManus** vs *Daniel* **Hicks** judgment for £ 3-10.

Jonathan **Owsley** vs *James* **Shackelford** continued.

William **Holland** vs *Thomas* **Roberds** judgment £ 4-10.

A report of a road from **Lewis** Mill to Boonsborough is returned and ordered recorded and David **England** is appointed surveyor of the above road and Aaron **Lewis**, gent. to lott the tithes.

Ordered that William **Irvine**, Thomas **Reynolds** and Archibald **Woods** or any two of them be appointed to settle and adjust the account between Harris **Massie** and the Sheriff of this County for the year 1787 and 1788 and that they meet at the house of William **Irvine** on the 25th of the present month and make report thereof to the next Court.

Ordered that the road from Madison Courthouse to John **Kincaid**, Junr. is discontinued.

Ordered that William **Kavanaugh** be recommended to his excellency the Governor as a proper person to act as Lieutenant in the Militia in this County.

Ordered that Robert **Moore** clear the road at Jesse **Embry's** agreeable to a late report.

Ordered that the Sheriff do summons a jury to ascertain the damages done to the lands of Samuel **Biggerstaff** by the road running through the same from the mouth of Jacks Creek to Collier's Warehouse and make report of the same.

On the motion of John **Snoddy**, Esqr., Sheriff, John **Hopkins** is appointed one of his deputies and took the oath accordingly.

Ordered that the Court adjourn until Court in Course.

George **Adams**

At a Court *of Quarter Session* held for Madison County on Tuesday the 2nd day of November 1790.

Present George **Adams**, James **Barnett**, Archibald **Woods** and Aaron **Lewis**, gent.

An inventory and appraisement of the estate of James **Black**, deceased returned and ordered recorded.

A deed from Joseph **Bledsoe** to John **Bailey** was proved by oaths of Aaron **King** and Mary **Dyer** and ordered to be certified.

Green **Clay**, foreman; George **Boone**, John **Anderson**, Thomas **Kennedy**, Leonard **Hetherly**, William **Williams**, William **Calk**, James **McDaniels**, John **Kincaid**, Samuel **Boyd**, Edward [*Edmund*] **Williams**, Edward **Turner**, Joseph **Scott**, Robert **Kirkpatrick**, Zacheriah **Dozier**, Samuel **Freeman** a Grand Jury for this County was sworn having received their charge retired to consider of the presentments.

Edmund **Terrill**, Captain; Joe **Logsdon**, Lieutenant; James **Fennell** appeared and took the oath required by Law as officers of Militia in this County.

Present John **Boyle**, gent.

A report of a settlement between Harris **Massie** and the Sheriff of this County was returned and ordered recorded.

Ordered that Barney **Stagner** be recommended to his Excellency the Governor as a proper person to serve as Lieutenant in the Militia for this County and John **Jackson** Ensign, also John **Prator** as Captain, John **Slavin** Lieutenant, and Closs **Thompson** Ensign.

The grand jury returned and made the following report. We of the Grand Jury having retired and made due inquiry into the serveral duties required of our body do find no presentments to report.

A report of a road from **Woodes** and **Carpenters** Mill to where it intersects the Boonsborough Road and where the Jacks Creek road Comes in is established and ordered recorded. Ordered that John **White** be appointed surveyor of the same and Archibald **Woods**, gent. to lott of the tithes to work on the same.

Madison County, Kentucky Court Order Book A   105

A deed from William **Miller** and *Nancy his wife* to Michael **Wallace** was proved by the oath of George **Adams** and ordered to be certified.

A deed from Green **Clay** to Valentine **Stone** was acknowledged and ordered recorded.

Commonwealth vs *Peter* **Taylor** continued.

Same vs Same continued.

Same vs A*lexander* **Reid** continued

Same vs *James* **Martin** not *guilty* and continued.

Same vs *David* **Hall** dismissed.

Same vs J*ohn* **Reid** dismissed.

Same vs *James* **Robertson** judgment for 5 shillings and costs.

Same vs *James* **Robertson** judgment for 5 shillings and costs.

Ordered that John **Bruse** be appointed surveyor of the road in the room of Richard **Runnells**.

Ordered that John **Halley**, gent lott the tithes to work under Peter **Evans**.

Samuel **Bigerstaff** against *Samuel* **Hopper** the motion and oath of a dedimus is granted to take the deposition of John **Halley**.

John **Prater** a Captain, William **Kavanaugh** Lieutenant and William **Kerley** an Ensign took the oath required by Law.

Ordered that the court adjourn untill tomorrow 9 of the oclock.

George **Adams**

At a Court held for Madison County on Wednesday the 3rd day of November 1790.

Present George **Adams**, James **Barnett**, John **Boyles** and Archibald **Woods**, gent.

John **Holder** vs *William* **Hoy**, executors. *Sarefacious granted him against John* **South** *and Richard* **Tunstall***, executors.*

James **Hogan** assee *of John* **Colson** vs Same. Same.

William **Bush** vs *John* **Halley** dismissed with costs.

John **Holley** to pay John **Wilkinson** [*Wilkerson*] and John **Hopper**, Gary **Allen** against **Bush**.

Jonathan **Gillit**, Esqr. produced a License as attorney at Law and took the oaths proscribed by Law.

Frederick **Raperdan** vs *William* **Smith** and *William* **Simpson**. Jury sworn to inquire *damages* towit. Joseph **Moore**, Jesse **May**, John **Black**, Robert **Dean**, Anthony **Rogers**, James **Stephenson**, George **Finley**, Jeremiah **Perry**, James **McKinney**, Peter **Taylor**, William **Creath**, James **McAlister**. Returned verdict for the plaintiff. Damages £ 2-6-10½.

Richard **Hickman** vs *Andrew* **Banks** and *Edmund* **Hockaday** payment joined.

Benjamin **Northcut** by *George Adams* vs *Luke* **Moore** continued.

Andrew **Banks** abates and return. *Andrew Banks is no inhabitant of this county.*

Richard **Hickman** vs *Edmund* **Hockaday** to try the issue towit. Charles **Campbell**, Andrew **Donalson**, Cornelius **Daugherty**, Moses **Faris**, Joseph **Proctor**, Alexander **Reid**, John **Clark**, Sarshal **Cooper**, Robert **Braden**, John **Steel**, Matthew **Sims**, Randol **Sims**. Returned verdict for the plaintiff and damages £ 101-5.

George **Boyds** vs *Thomas* **Batts**. Jury sworn to inquire of damages towit. Joseph **Moore**, Jesse **May**, John **Black**, Robert **Dean**, Anthony **Rodgers**, James **Stephenson**, George **Finley**, Jeremiah **Perry**, Joseph **McKinny**, William **Butcher**, Andrew **Kennedy** and Humphrey **Best**. Returned verdict for plaintiff. Damages £ 37-8.

Charles **Boyd** vs *Thomas* **Batts** continued at defendants costs.

George **Boyd** to pay Hardy **Rolls** 3 days attendance and 72 miles vs **Batts**. Also James **Coghill** 3 days attendance and 83 miles vs **Batts**. Also Jonathan **Owsley** 3 days attendance vs *Thomas* **Batts**.

Nathan **Huston** vs *Zachariah* **Dozier** continued at plaintif costs.

On the motion and oath of Nathan **Huston** a dedimus is awarded to take the deposition of Hugh **Logan** debeneese vs *Zachariah* **Dozier**.

Present David **Gass**, gent.

Nathan **Huston** to pay Hugh **Logan** one days attendance and 60 miles vs **Dozier**.

William **Harrison** vs *Zachariah* **Dozier** continued.

Zachariah **Dozier** to pay Solomon **Shoemaker** 2 days attendance and 80 miles also Isaac **Garvin** the same. Also Mary **Huston** the same against **Huston**.

Thomas **Kennedy** vs *Robert* **Dean** continued.

Samuel **Hopper** vs *Samuel* **Biggerstaff** continued at defendants costs.

Madison County, Kentucky Court Order Book A   107

John **Weldon** and ux vs *Robert* **Adams** continued.
John **Barnett** vs *Andrew* **Donelson** continued plaintiff costs.
Robert **Adams** vs *Joseph* **Weldon** and ux continued.
Azariah **Martin** and *John* **Bruce** continued.
Patrick **Gallihar** vs *John* **Martin** dismissed at defendants costs. *In trespass, assault and battery.*
Harris **Massie** vs *David* **Lynch** continued.
Samuel **Hopper** to pay Elizabeth **Williams** three days attendance also Prudence **Davis** 2 days attendance vs **Biggerstaff**.
Ordered that James **Barnett** and Archibald **Woods** be added in addition to the Commissioners appointed to toll Richard **Hickman** and Lydia his wife the dower of the said Lydia as widow of Christopher **Irvine**, deceased any three of them to make report.
William **Caldwell** vs *James* **Mathews** jury sworn to enquire of damages towit: Cornelius **Daughterty**, Alex **Reed**, James **McAlister**, Moses **Faris**, Joseph **Proctor**, Robert **Braden**, John **Steel**, Mathew **Sims**, Sarshall **Cooper**, James **Stephenson**, Samuel **Brown**, Joseph **McKinney** returned verdict for plaintiff £ 10 damages.
John **Fitzjerrall** vs *Jeremiah* **Perry** dismissed.
Ordered that a writ of adquodamnun issue to take the valuation of the land of Samuel **Biggerstaff** thro which the road leading from mouth of Jacks Creek to Collier's Warehouse runs and return an inquistion of the true value of the land of the said **Bickerstaff** taken up by the said road to mitts on the 17th day of this inst. on the lands.
William **Morrison** produced a Commission appointing him Captain in the Militia of this County whereupon he took the oaths prescribed by Law.
Charles **Campbell** vs *Humphrey* **Best** continued.
Zachariah **Dozier** to pay Cornelius **Daughterty** one day attendance against *Nathan* **Huston**.
Zachariah **Dozier** to pay *Jeremiah* **Perry** 1 day against *Nathan* **Huston**.
Ordered that the Court adjourn until Court in Course.
       David **Gass**

At a Court held for Madison County on Tuesday the 7th day of December 1790.

Present George **Adams**, David **Gass**, Archibald **Woods**, Aaron **Lewis**, Moses **Dooley** and Charles **Debrell**, gent.

A statement of the County Levy 1790

To the Clerk for Exoficio Services	1500
To the sheriff for ditto.	1500
To the State[*Commonwealth*] Attorney ditto	1200
To Alexander **Denny** for 1 grown woolf	100
John **Kaid** ditto.	100
To Thomas **Black** for three ditto.	300
To Andrew **Black** for 1 ditto.	100
To Adam **Woods** for three ditto.	100
To Clerk for his services to appoint Commissions and examining their books	1000
To Samuel **Cochran** for making Stocks and Pillery &c	1280
To Aaron **Lewis** for his *public services*	50
To Clerk for attending Call Court	200
To the Sheriff for summoning ditto.	200
To a deposition	6628
To Sheriff Commission for Collecting	942
Credit by tithes 1440 at 10 pounds Tob each	14400

Present James **Barnett** gent.

A power of attorney between William **Hicks** and Flanders **Callaway** acknowledged by James **Boggs** and ordered recorded.

A deed from William **Hicks** *and Daniel Boone* to *James Boggs* was acknowledged *by Flanders Callaway their attorney* and ordered recorded.

A deed from William Hicks to Thomas Massie was acknowledged by James Boggs his attorney and ordered recorded.

A deed from the same to David **Gentry** was acknowledged *by James Boggs* and ordered recorded.

A deed from the same to Jacob **Pattison** was acknowledged *by James Boggs* and ordered recorded.

A deed from James **Bryant** attorney in fact of James **Smith** was proved by the oaths of Joseph **Titus**, John **Sawyers**, John **Knox** and ordered recorded.

A deed from Henry **Fields** to *Isaac* **Burgin** was proved by the oath of David **Crews** and ordered certified.

An instrument of writing from William **Hicks** revoking his power to James **Boggs** was proved oaths of John **McWilliams** and Benjamin **Titsworth** witnesses thereto and ordered recorded.

A deed from the executors of Richard **Henderson**, deceased to William **Goodloe** is ordered to be recorded by a probate from the Clerk of Granville County.

A deed from William **Hicks** to John **Hunt** was proved by the oaths of John **McWilliams** and Benjamin **Titsworth** and ordered recorded. Certified.

Letters of administration is granted to Patsey **Hoy** and John **Glover** on the estate of Roland **Hoy**, deceased and entered into bond conditioned as the Law directs also took the oaths required. Securities are John **South** and Aaron **Lewis**. Ordered that David **Crews**, Aaron **Lewis**, William **Jones** and Samuel **South** or any three of them first sworn do appraise the estate of Rowland **Hoy**, deceased.

Ordered that John **Gass** be appointed surveyor of the road in room of John **Wilson**.

Letters of administration granted Francis **Williams** and William **Jones** on the estate of Isaac **Williams**, deceased and entered into bond conditioned as the law directs and took the oaths required. *Securities are Richard **Tunstall** and John **Glover**.* Ordered that James **Martin**, David **Crews**, Oswald **Towns** and William **Bardges**[*Bridges*] or any three of them being first sworn do appraise the estate of Isaac **Williams**, deceased.

John **South** vs *Jesse* **Hodges** *and Thomas* **Crews** dismissed.

A deed from Caleb **Callaway** to Christopher **Harris** proved by the oath of David **Gass** and John **Mitchell** and ordered certified.

On motion of Nicholas **Hawkins** his ear mark an underkeel in each ear in ordered recorded.

Charles **Campbell** vs *Humphrey* **Best** dismissed with costs.

Samuel **Brown** vs *Elisha* **Brooks** judgment £ 3.

Humphrey **Best** to pay John **Anderson** 5 days attendance against Charles **Campbell**. Same to pay John **Weldon** and Stephen **Best** fifteen days also to **Weldon** and *Stephen* **Best** 4 days **against** *Charles* **Campbell**.

Samuel **Brown** to pay Sarchall and Bracton **Coopers** 6 days each vs **Brooks**.

Alexander **Reed** to pay Joseph and Nicholas **Proctor** 6 days each vs **Dean**.

Elisha **Brooks** to Irvin **Jones** 2 days attendance against **Brown**. Same to pay David **Crews** 3 days against same.

Order that Court be adjourn until Court in Course.

James **Barnett**

At a Court held for Madison County on Tuesday the 4th day of January 1791.

Present David **Gass**, James **Barnett**, Archibald **Woods**, Joseph **Kennedy** and Moses **Dooley**, gent.

An inventory and appraisment of the estate of Isaac **Williams**, deceased is returned and ordered recorded.

A deed from Martin **Daniel** attorney in fact for Robert **Daniel** to Thomas **McClure** was proved by the oaths of John **Clark** and Abraham **Stevens** and Thomas **Lewis** and ordered recorded.

A deed from same to Thomas **Lewis** was proved by the oaths of John **Clark**, Thomas **McClure** and Abraham **Stevens** and ordered recorded.

An inventory and appraisement of the estate of Rowland **Hoy**, deceased was returned and ordered recorded.

On the motion of Harris **Massie** judgment is granted him against John **Snoddy**, gent., Sheriff of this County, for £ 10-8-9.

A deed from Caleb **Callaway** to Benjamin **Pursley** was proved by the oaths of James **French**, John **Farwell**, William **Antrobus** and ordered recorded.

A deed from Caleb **Callaway** to Thomas **Hart** was proved by the oaths of James **French**, William **Antriobus** and Benjamin **Persel** & ordered recorded.

James **French**, gent. named in the Commission of the peace for this County came into Court and took the oath of fidelity to the Commonwealth and the oath of a Justice of the Peace and present *took his seat accordingly*.

Ordered that John **Lewis**, William **Cooley**, Clemment **Hill** and Abraham **Stephens** or any three of them do view a way for a road from Fredergil **Adams'** Mill to the line of Lincoln County in order to intersect the Hickman and Sugar Creek Roads at their forks near John **Bryant's**.

Madison County, Kentucky Court Order Book A 111

Ordered that Jonathan **Gillet** have leave to build a house 16 feet square on the north corner of the public ground for an office for himself and to revert to the use of this Court as soon as it is not applied to that use.

A receipt from William **Hoy** to John **South** was proved by oaths of John **Glover** and Charles **Reynolds** witnesses thereto & ordered recorded.

Andrew **Hare** vs *William* **Harris** judgment for Plaintiff act. *£ 3-11-4 and costs.*

Absent Charles **Debrell**, gent.

Allen **Burton** vs *Charles* **Dibrell** continued for defendant.

A deed from William **Hicks** to John **Hunt** was fully proved by the oath Basil **Hunt** and ordered recorded.

John **Goggin** gent. named in the Commission of Peace for this County came into Court and took the oath of fidelity to the Commonwealth and the oath of a Justice of the Peace.

Present [blank]

James **Wilkinson** asee vs *Harris* **Massie** judgment per note. *£ 5 and costs.*

Walter **Beal** vs *William* **Orear** judgment for note. *£ 3-13-6 and costs.*

Matthew **Logan** vs *Edward* **McCoy** abates by defendant death.

Ordered that Flanagan **Graham** be appointed constable for this County.

Ordered that Page **Portwood** be appointed surveyor of the road from Carr **Smiths** to where Aquillas Road crosses the said road and that Archibald **Woods**, gent. do allott the hands to work on the same.

Ordered that Peter **Woods** do survey and clear the same road from Aquillas road to Archibald **Woods**.

Alexander **Reid** vs *Robert* **Dean** for judgment £ 2-10 and costs.

Ordered that Alex **Reid** pay Joseph **Proctor** one day vs *Robert* **Dean**.

Alexander **Reed** to pay Nicholas **Proctor** 1 day attendance.

Ordered that Court be adjourn until Court in Course.

David **Gass**

At a Court of Quarter Sessions held for Madison County at the Courthouse on Tuesday the 1st day of February 1791.

Present George **Adams**, James **Barnett**, Joseph **Kennedy** and Moses **Dooley**, gent.

A deed from William **Montgomery** to Robert **Brank** was proved by oaths of Thomas **Kennedy**, Joseph **Kennedy** and Andrew **Kennedy** and ordered recorded.

Michael **McNeely**, foreman; Thomas **Kennedy**, Andrew **Kennedy**, Isaac **Offe**, Andrew **Bogey**, John **Davis**, Andrew **Harris**, Edward **Taylor**, George **Hinton**, John **Anderson**, John **Kincaid**, William **Hancock**, Edward **Williams**, Hugh **Campbell**, Peter **Taylor**, William **Briscoe** and David **Gentry** was sworn a Grand Jury for this County, received their charge and retired to consider.

Thomas **Kennedy** vs *Robert* **Deane**. Samuel **Estill** special bail.

Inventory and appraisment of the estate of Edward[*Elizabeth*] **Stephenson** returned and ordered recorded.

Thomas **Montgomery** named in Commission of the Peace for this County took the oaths of office and the oath to the United States and his seat as a Magistrate.

David **Gass**, gent. produced a commission appointing him Sheriff of this County who took the several oaths of office and the oath to the United States and entered into and acknowledged bonds with William **Irvine**, James **Barnett**, Joseph **Kennedy** and John **Snoddy** his securities.

Present Aaron **Lewis** and John **Goggin**, gent.

On motion of David **Gass**, gent., Sheriff John **Gass** and John **Hopkins** qualified as his deputies.

A deed from Green **Clay** and Jesse **Hodges** to Peter **Evans** was proved by oaths of David **England**, William **Orear** and Tobias **James** and ordered recorded.

On the motion of Edmund **Hockaday** a judgment is granted him for one hundred and one pounds and five shillings for damages and two hundred and seventeen pounds of tobacco and sixteen shillings and six pense for costs (being the sum recovered by Richard **Hickman** vs said **Hockaday** as security for Andrew **Banks**) vs **Banks** and the costs of this motion.

William **Stuart** vs *Isaac* **Ingram**. Joseph **Kennedy** special bail.

The Grand Jury returned and presents William **Young** of Milford Town for fighting and for profane swearing expressed in these words (by God). Also Thomas **Jacobs** for fighting . And having nothing further to present were discharged.

Order that process Issue against the persons presented today. *Issue summons.*

A power of attorney from David **Tanner** and *Mary his wife* to John **Halley** proved by John **Halley**, William **Wilkinson** [*Wilkerson*] and ordered recorded.

Jacob **Repheart** vs Samuel **Harris** dismissed at defendant costs in two suits.

Wilkinson [*Wilkerson*] asse vs *John Adams and William* **Orear** Peter **Evans** special bail.

Ordered that John **Halley**, gent. be added to the Commission ordered to view and keep in repair the scales and weights at **Collier's** Whearhouse.

David **Gass**, gent., Sheriff of this County and complained of the unsufficiency of the jaile.

A deed from Thomas **Kennedy** to Andrew **Bogey** was acknowledged and ordered recorded.

Commonwealth vs Peter **Taylor** dismissed.

Same vs Same Same.

John **Barnett** vs *Andrew* **Donalson** jury to try issue viz. *In trespass, assault and battery.* Samuel **Boyd**, John **Carpenter**, William **Pollard**, Nicholas **Hawkins**, James **Boggs**, Barney **Stagner**, James **Berry**, Benjamin **Duncan**, Samuel **Burton**, William **Barnett**, William **Creath** and William **Coughran** returned verdict 45 shillings damages.

Samuel **Hopper** *by William* **Hopper** *his father and next friend* vs *Samuel* **Bigerstaff** dismissed agreed. *In trespass, assault and battery.*

Benjamin **Northcutt** *by George Adams his next friend* vs *Luke* **Moore** dismissed agreed.

Samuel **Bigerstaff** pay William **Oakley** 5 days, James **Hill** 4 days, David **McWilliams** 3 days against **Hopper**.

Charles **Boyd** vs *Thomas* **Batts** continued for defendant.

William **Harrison** vs *Zachariah* **Dozier** continued.

Azariah **Martin** vs *John* **Bruse** continued.

Ordered that Court adjourn till 9 oclock tomorrow.

George **Adams**

At a Court continued and held for Madison County on Wednesday the 2nd day of February 1791.

Present George **Adams**, James **Barnett**, Charles **Dibrell**, James **French**, John **Goggin**, gent.

On motion of Charles **Campbell** by his attorney an injunction is granted him to stay proceedings on a judgment obtained against him by Humphrey **Best** in this Court and he is to enter into bond in the Clerk's office with Thomas **Todd** his security.

A deed from John **Hunt** to Samuel **Black** was proved by the oaths of John **Black**, Benjamin **Duncan** and Joseph **Hawkins** and ordered recorded.

On motion of Thomas **Batts** to obtain an injunction against George **Boyd** it is the opinion of this Court that the bill be rejected.

Barney **Stagner** vs Trustees of Harrodsburg injunction decreed perpetual.

Thomas **Kennedy** vs *Robert* **Deane** continued.

John **Weldon** and ux vs *Robert* **Adams** continued.

Robert **Adams** vs *Joseph* **Weldon** and ux continued.

Thomas **Batts** exempted from pay levy for one negro man named Joe was aged and infirm.

Commonwealth vs *James* **Martin** dismissed.

Eusebrius **Hubbard** appointed guardian to Reubin, Gehue and George **Estis** orphans of Richard **Estis** and he entered into and acknowledged bond with Benjamin **Duncan** his security in the penalty of £ 100 conditioned as the Law directs.

Present John **Miller**, gent.

Nathan **Huston** vs *Zachariah* **Dozier** continued for defendant.

John **Woods** vs *William* **Hoy's** executors. Jury sworn to inquire towit. William **Creath**, James **Boggs**, Robert **Knox**, Benjamin **Duncan**, William **Kerly**, John **Black**, John **Mitchell**, Barney **Stagner**, Evan **Watson**, Alex **Reid**, William **Woods** and Michael **Farris** returned verdict for plaintiff £ 180 damages.

On the motion of Zach **Dozier** a dedimus is granted him to take the depostition of Solomon **Shoemaker** against *Nathan* **Huston**.

Fanny **English** vs *Jesse* **May** continued.

John **Mathews** assee vs *Jesse* **May** jury sworn to judgment and towit. Thomas **Warren**, William **Ham**, Samuel **Black**, Harris **Massie**, David **Massie**, James **Stephenson**, Allen **Burton**, Abraham **Burton**, Cary **Phelps**, Francis **McNut**, Cornelius **Daughterty** and Jeremiah **Perry** returned a verdict for plaintiff £ 20 damages. *Plaintiff sustained damages by non performance of a certain contract.*

Harris **Massie** vs David **Lynch** continued.

Richard **Runnals** vs Joseph **Brown** continued.

James **Boggs** vs John **Hunt** and William **Hicks** rule to advertise against **Hicks** and that he enter his appearance on or before the 1st Tuesday in August next. *Hicks is no inhabitant of this state.*

James **McNutt** vs Robert **Dean** writ inquiry set aside a tinder pleaded and continued. *Defendant says he did tender the property in the declaration mentioned.*

John **South** vs Jonathan **Owsley** and James **Shackelford** by jury to inquire of &c towit. Benjamin **Duncan**, William **Kerley**, John **Black**, Alex **Reid**, Robert **Knave**, Andrew **Miller**, James **Boggs**, Barney **Stagner**, William **Creath**, Evan **Watson**, Andrew **Kennedy**, Michael **Farris** returned verdict for plaintiff £ 7-10 damages.

Harry **Innes** vs *Michael* **McNeely** discontinued.

John **Tanner** vs *Higgason* **Grubbs** continued.

Same vs Same same.
Same vs Same same.
Same vs Same same.
Same vs Same same.
Same vs Same same.
Same vs Same same.
Same vs Same same.
Same vs Same same.
Same vs Same same.

King vs **Bank** same.

William **Jones** asee vs *Aquilah* **White** continued.

Nicholas **Conrad** vs *Jesse* **May** dismissed.

Thomas **Pasley** vs *Leonard* **Dozier** continued.

Ordered that Joseph **Bramwell** be appointed Constables. And Thomas Daniell.

Zachariah **Dozier** to pay Solomon **Shoemaker** 2 days *and 80 miles.* Isaac **Garvin**, Mary **Huston** 2 days vs **Huston** forty miles each going and coming.

Allen **Burton** vs *Charles* **Debrille** judgment £ 1-10.

Peter **Taylor** vs *William* **Jones** dismissed.

Zachariah **Dozier** to pay Cornelius **Daughterty** 1 day against *Nathan* **Huston**.

Allen **Burton** to pay Philip **Williams**, Sherod **Willis** & Richard **Barrow** 1 day each vs *Charles* **Dibrell**.

David **Bullock** asee vs *Anthony* **Rogers** continued.

Ordered that Court be adjourn until Court in Course.

George **Adams**

At a Court held for Madison County on Tuesday the 4th day of March 1791.

Present George **Adams**, Archibald **Woods**, Robert **Rodes** and Thomas **Montgomery**.

On motion of John **Prator** his ear mark a crop and a slit in the left and a swallow fork and under bitt in the right is ordered recorded.

Power of attorney from Samuel **Anderson** to John **Stephenson** was acknowledged and ordered to be recorded.

Upon the motion of Samuel **Shackelford**, Junr. ordered that he be permitted to keep a tavern in the Town of Milford on his entering into bond with Jonathan **Gillett** his security as the Law directs.

Deed from Henry **Fields** to Isaac **Burgin** proved by oath of John **Crook** and ordered to be certified.

Deed from Nicholas **Welch** to James **Thompson** proved by the oaths of Alexander **Boyle**, Joseph **Henderson** and Moses **Dooley** and ordered to be recorded.

Deed from William **Dryden** and Mary his wife to John **Young** acknowledged by said William and ordered recorded.

Ordered that Aaron **Lewis**, gent. be appointed to lay off the hands to work on the road from David **Woodrough's** to the three mile tree.

Present James **French**, gent. Absent James **Barnett**, gent. Present John **Miller**, Aaron **Lewis** and Moses **Dooley**.

Ordered that John **Miller** be appointed Colonel, William **Irvine**, Lieutenant Colonel and Samuel **Estill**, Major to the 2nd Batalion.

Sarah **Hoy** widow and relict of William **Hoy**, deceased and came into court and relinquished all benefit or claim to the provision made for her in her said husband's will and claims the thirds of his estate.

Madison County, Kentucky Court Order Book A   117

Jesse **Noland** appointed surveyor in the room of James **Hendricks** and Benjamin **Cooper** in the room of John **Jackson**.

Deed and commission from Thomas **Kennedy** and *Agnes his wife* to Andrew **Bogey** return ordered recorded. Being before acknowledged.

William **Turpin** vs *Henry* **Laughlin** dismissed agreed.

A report of the place for building the whearhouse at Boonsborough was returned and ordered recorded.

Ordered that Moses **Dooley** be recommended to his Excellency as Captain and James **Black** as Lieutenant.

Ordered that John **Sappington**, Benjamin **Pursley**, Peter **Evans** and William **Calk** view a way for a road from opposite John **Holder's** boatyard to where it may most conveniently intersect the road from Boonsborough to Madison Courthouse and make report.

Order that Court adjourn until Court in Course.

George **Adams**

At a Court held for Madison County on Tuesday the 4th day of April 1791.

Present George **Adams**, John **Boyle**, Archibald **Woods** and Robert **Rodes**, Gent.

John **Pitman** qualified as deputy sheriff.

Ordered that a summons issue to James **McCollister** to shew cause why he should not be fined for a certain contempt offered to this Court by leading his horse thro diferent parts of this Courthouse &c and also same to issue for witnesses to appear and give testimony to the above charge returnable to next Court.

Ordered that the Sheriff purchase a lock &c for the purpose of securing the Courthosue.

Ordered that Court be adjourned till Court in Course.

George **Adams**

At a Court of Quarter Sessions held at Madison Courthouse on 3rd day of May 1791.

Present George **Adams**, James **Barnett**, Archibald **Woods**, Joseph **Kennedy**, Aaron **Lewis** and Moses **Dooley**, gent.

Michael **McNeely**, foreman; Thomas **Kennedy**, Andrew **Kennedy**, Ambrose **Ross**, Stephen **Merritt**, Lofty **Pullins**, Baziel **Maxwell**, John **Moberly**, Abraham **Newland**, James **Martin**, Samuel **Estill**, Edward **Turner**, John **McLean**, William **Goodloe**, James **Johnson**, Peter **Taylor** and David **Gentry** were sworn a Grand Jury for this County having received their charge retired to consider of their presentments.

James I. **Dozier's** last will and testament was proved by oaths of Aaron **Lewis** and Weldon **South** witnesses thereto and ordered recorded. Zachriah and Leonard **Dozier** qualified as executors named in the last will and testament of James I. **Dozier**, deceased and acknowledged bond in penalty of £ 200 with James **Montgomery** and William **Williams** their securities conditioned as the Law directs.

Thomas **Davis**, Esqr is permitted to practice as an attorney at Law whereupon he took the oaths required by Law.

A deed from John **Hunt** to William **Estill** proved by James **Anderson**, Jonathan **Gillett** and Samuel **Shackelford** and ordered recorded.

A power of attorney from William **Creath** to Samuel **Small** acknowledged and ordered recorded.

Ordered that Peter **Evans**, Thomas **Sutherland**, Page **Portwood**, William **Jones** or any three of them be appointed appraisers of the personal estate of James I. **Dozier**, deceased.

David **Gentry**, Sen. excused from his personal County service [*levies*].

The Grand Jury returned into Court and made the following presentments.

Solomen **Asbell** for profane swearing at Jeremiah **Crews** on the 28th day of April last for saying God dam your dog and Walter **Middleton** for the same by say by God, at Paint Lick on the 11th of April last. It is ordered that they be summoned.

Jacob **Stearns** is appointed to build the wherehouse at Boonsborough whereupon he entered into bond.

Ordered that James **McAllister** be fined in the sum of ten pounds for a certain contempt offered to this Court by leading his horse through different parts of the Courthouse.

Letters of Administration is granted to William **Irvine** on the estate of Thomas **Reynolds**, deceased, whereupon he took the oath required by Law.

A deed from Alexander **Reed** to Mary **Graham** acknowledged and ordered recorded.

Commonwealth vs *William* **Young** dismissed.
Same vs *Thomas* **Jacobs** ditto.
Same vs *Alexander* **Reed** ditto.
Charles **Boyd** vs *Thomas* **Batts** continued.
William **Harrison** vs *Zachariah* **Dozier** same.
Thomas **Kennedy** vs *Robert* **Dean** continued.
John **Weldon** and ux vs *Robert* **Adams** same.
Robert **Adams** vs *Joseph* **Weldon** and ux same.
Azariah **Martin** vs *John* **Bruce** same.

Nathan **Huston** vs *Zachariah* **Dozier** continued for defendant and ruled for trial on the first day of the next Court.

Ordered that the following rule be established in the proceedings in Chancery in suits commenced vs absent defendants and others residing in this Country viz. That such absentees enter their appearance with the Clerk of this Court or in open court within nine months from the return day of the *subpoena* and then to conform to the further rules and orders of this Court.

James **Boggs** vs *John* **Hicks** and *William* **Hunt**. The defendant **Hicks** not having entered his appearance ordered that the same be advertised accoring to Law and that he enter his appearance agreeable to the rule of this Court.

Aaron **Lewis** vs *Boud* **Estill** dedimus to take the deposition of Lofty **Pullen** on the motion and affidavit of defendant.

James **McNutt** vs *Robert* **Deane** jury to try issue viz. William **Calk**, Thomas **Massie**, Richard **Gentry**, James **Berry**, William **Creath**, John **Mitchell**, Joseph **Ham**, James **Boggs**, Harris **Massie**, Evan **Watson**, John **Starns** and Alexander **Off** and returned verdict and for reasons appearing were discharged.

David **Gentry** vs *William* **Hicks** and *John* **Hunt** same order as **Boggs** vs **Hicks** &c.

Jacob **Patten** vs Same same order.

Thomas **Massie** vs Same same.

Thomas **Pasley** vs **Dozier** continued.

John **Tanner** vs *Higgason* **Grubbs** in ten suits continued.

Aaron **King** vs *Thomas* **Banks** judgment and note and costs. £ 4-6.

William **Jones** assee vs *Aquilla* **White** judgment for £ 3 and costs.

Samuel **Dedman** vs *Ebenezer* **Brooks** dismissed at defendant costs accept attorney fee.

David **Bullock** asee vs *Anthony* **Rodgers** £ 3 and costs.
William **Murry** vs *William* **Moore** continued.
John **Martin** vs *David* **Noble** judgment per note and costs. £ 2-6.
John **Leveridge** vs *Daniel* **Nichols** continued.
William **Watson** vs *James* **Barnett** discontinued.
Zachariah **Dozier** against *Nathan* **Huston**. Hugh **Logan** claims 1 day and 30 miles traveling.
James **Greenlee** vs *James* **Nicholson** als. sums.
Andrew **McCalla** vs *John* **Harris** als sums.
James **McNutt** vs *Robert* **Dean** dedimus to take the deposition of Edward **Russell** for plaintiff.
Edward **Williams** vs *Elisha* **Brooks** continued.
Ordered that the order of today leving a fine of ten pounds vs James **McCallister** be set aside and that the attorney for the County file an *indictment* vs him for the said contempt at the next Grand Jury Court.
Ordered that the following rates be established within this County.

Rum at . . . . 12 shillings per gallon
Whiskey . . . . 8p per gallon
Bear at . . . . 1/4 ditto.
Corn or oats at . . . . 3 pence per pottle.
Dinner . . . . 1 shilling 3 pence.
Breakfast and Supper at . . . . 9 pence each.
Pasturage of stablage at . . . . 9 pence for 12 hours.
Lodging . . . . 6 pence.

Ordered that Mathew **Adams** be appointed Captain in the room of Jonathan **Owsley**.
Ordered that Court adjourn till Court in Course.

George **Adams**

At a Court held for Madison County on Tuesday the 7th day of June 1791.
Present George **Adams**, James **Barnett**, Robert **Rodes** and John **Miller**, gent.

Madison County, Kentucky Court Order Book A 121

A deed from Green **Clay** to Andrew **Bogey** was proved by the oaths of Benjamin **Wheeler**, Andrew **Bogey**, Junr. and James **Bogey** and ordered recorded.

A deed from Richard **Cave** and *Elizabeth his wife* to Mary **Crawford** was proved by the oaths of Charles **Bland** and Thomas **McClure** and ordered certified.

Letters of Administration is grant to Mathew **Sims** and *Elizabeth his wife* on the estate of John **Night** whereupon they entered into bond conditioned at the Law directs and. *Securities are Jesse Embry and Thomas Jones.*

A deed and comm. from Thomas **Kennedy** and *Agnes his wife* to Andrew **Bogey** and ordered recorded.

Oaths required by Law and Jesse **Embry**, Edward **Turner**, Nicholas **White**, Aswell **Towns** appraisers.

Ordered that James **Stephenson**, Robert **Knox**, Jesse **Huston** and Samuel **Morrow** view the way for a road from this to **Hawkin's** Mill.

A deed from John **Huntt** to William **Estill** was proved by Samuel **Estill**, Thomas **Black**, and Samuel **Shackelford** and ordered recorded.

A deed from the same to John **McWilliams** proved by the oaths of John **Estill**, John and Samuel **Shackelford** and ordered recorded.

A deed from John **Brent** to Robert **Clark**, Junr. proved by oaths of Robert **Clark**, Sr., Bennett **Clark** and Mary **Rowland** and ordered recorded.

A deed from James **Knox** attorney for Alexander **Sinclair** to Bennett **Pemberton** proved by Thomas **Montgomery**, John **Carson**, John **Smith** and ordered recorded.

A deed from Bennett **Pemberton** to Charles **Ballew** was proved by Thomas **Montgomery**, John **Smith**, North **East** and ordered recorded.

A deed from same to North **East** proved by Thomas **Montgomery**, Charles **Bellew**, John **Carson** and ordered recorded.

Same from same to John **Smith** proved by the same witnesses and ordered recorded.

A deed from James **Knox**, attorney in fact for Alexander **Sinclear**, to Thomas **Montgomery** was proved by Charles **Ballew**, John **Smith**, North **East** and ordered recorded.

A deed from North **East** to John **Carson** was acknowledged and ordered recorded.

A deed from William **Dryden** and ux to William **Creath** was proved by James **Anderson**, John **Gass**, Benjamin **Duncan** and ordered recorded.

Inventory and appraisement of the estate of James I. **Dozier** returned and ordered recorded.

Thomas **Land** is exempted from pay County and parish levies *by age and infirmity.*

On the motion of Joel **Hill** his ear mark a swallows fork in the left ear and under keel in the right is ordered recorded.

Ordered that Joel **Hill** be appointed surveyor of the road in room of David **Hall**.

A deed from Robert **Fleming** to Joseph **Phelps** was proved by oaths of Joel **Embry** and ordered certified.

Edward **Williams** vs *Elisha* **Brooks** judgment for £ 2-5 and costs.

Edward **Williams** to pay Thomas **Hoper** 2 days attendance vs *Elisha* **Brooks**.

A deed from John **Woods** and *Abigail his wife* to Joseph **Ellison** acknowledged and ordered recorded. femme relinquished.

James **McDaniel** is appointed surveyor in room of David **Crews**.

On the motion and oath of James **Stephenson** dedimus to take the deposition of Joshua **Abner** Debeniesse vs *William* **Robinson** [*Robertson*].

Ordered that the Sheriff summon Lawrence **Thompson** and John **Lutterell** to show cause why if any a road *from opposite* **Holder's** *boatyard* may not past through their land.

A deed from William **Jones** and *Mary his wife* to James **Anderson** acknowledged & ordered recorded. fem relinquished.

On motion of Thomas **Lewis** didimus to take the deposition of Henry **McCleyea** [*McElyary*] vs Zephah **Murphy**.

Ordered that William **Kavanaugh** and Samuel **South** be recommended as Captain also Asa **Searcy** and Daniel **Williams** as Lieutenants also Samuel **Barton**, David **Gentry**, Zachariah **Davis** and Thomas **Turner** as Ensigns.

Ordered that Richard **Hickman** be allowed nine pounds for the board of the three orphans of Christopher **Irvine**, deceased for one year and that the guardians of the said children pay the same.

Ordered that Court adjourn until Court in Course.

George **Adams**

Madison County, Kentucky Court Order Book A   123

At a Court held for Madison Courthouse on Tuesday the 16th day of June 1791 for the examination of William **Kincaid** charged with feloniously robing the storehouse of Samuel **Estill** of sundry goods before the worshipful George **Adams**, James **Barnett**, Archibald **Woods**, Robert **Rodes** and John **Miller**, gent. the said William **Kincaid** having appeared accordingly to his recognance and it being demanded of him whether he was guilty of the charge aforesaid or not says he is not guilty thereof whereof upon sundry evidence were sworn and examined and he heard in his own defense on consideration whereof it is the opinion of the Court that he be committed to jail and that he be sent for further tryal in the Superior Court.

George **Adams**

At a Court called and held at Madison Courthouse on Thursday the 16th day of January 1791. For the examination of Samuel **McCleary** charged with feloniously robing the storehouse of Samuel **Estill** of sundry goods before the worshipfull Court of George **Adams**, James **Barnett**, Archibald **Woods**, Robert **Rodes** and John **Miller**, gent. The said Samuel **McCleary** having appeared according to his recognizance and it being demanded of him whether he was guilty of the charge aforesaid or not says he is not guilty thereof whereup sundry evidence were sworn and examined and he heard in his own defense on consideration whereof it is the opinion of this Court that he *is not guilty and* be inlarged.

George **Adams**

At a Court called and held at Madison Courthouse on Thursday the 16th day of June 1791 for the examination of James **Herrin** charged with feloniously robing the storehouse of Samuel **Estill** of sundry goods before the worshipful Court of George **Adams**, James **Barnett**, Archibald **Woods**, Robert **Rodes** and John **Miller**, gent. the said James **Herrin** having appeared according to his recognance and it being demanded of him whether he was guilty thereof whereupon sundry evidences were examined and he heard in his own defence on consideration whereof it is the opinion of the Court that he appear at the next Grand Jury Court *to answer for a misdemeanor* whereupon the said James **Herrin** is bound to his Excellency the Governor in the sum of two hundred pounds and William **Crawford** and Robert **Kincaid** his surety in the sum of one hundred pounds each to be discharged by his appearance as above.

George **Adams**

Memorandum be it remember that Hardy **Bennett**, John **McMullen** and Alexander **McMullen** acknowledged themselves bound to his Excellency the Governor the sum of one hundred pounds each their heirs executors and administrators. to be discharged by their personally appearing at the Supreme Court for the District of Kentucky on the first day of next Supreme Court to be held for the said district. Then and there to give testimony against William **Kincaid** and to abid the further order of said Court.

George **Adams**

At a Court called and held at Madison Courthouse on Tuesday the 28th day of June 1791 for the examination of Hugh **Ross** charged with feloniously robing the storehouse of Samuel **Estill** of sundry goods before the worshipful George **Adams**, James **Barnett**, Archibald **Woods**, Robert **Rodes**, John **Miller** and James **French**, gent. The said Hugh **Ross** having appeared according to his recognizance and it being demanded of him whether he was guilty of the charge aforesaid or not says he is not thereof guilty whereupon sundry witnesses were sworn and examined and heard in his own defense on consideration whereof the opinion of the Court that he ought to be layed before the judges of the Supreme Court for the felony aforesaid and that he be remand to jail and from thence removed to the public jail in Danville.

Samuel **Estill**, William **Estill**, Abraham **Kimberlan**, John **Martin** and James **French** came into Court and acknowledged themselves severally bound to his Excellency, Beverly **Randolph**, Esqr. Governor of this Commonwealth in the sum of £ 100 each to be served and made of his several goods and chattels &c to be discharged by their personally appearing before the judges of the Supreme Court in Danville on the first Monday in October next and then to give testimony against Hugh **Ross** for felony and not to depart without leave of the Court.

George **Adams**

At a Court held for Madison on Tuesday the 5th day of July 1791.

Madison County, Kentucky Court Order Book A   125

Present George **Adams**, Archibald **Woods**, Aaron **Lewis**, Robert **Rodes**, John **Miller** and Thomas **Montgomery**, gent.

A deed from William **Kertley** to Elijah **Kertley** proved by the oaths John **Rogers**, James **Cowhert** and John **Kertly** and ordered recorded.

Ordered that Absolem **Crook** be exempted from paying County levy *by age and infirmity.*

Dedimus to take the depostion of Sherwood **Harris**, Zachariah **Wilburn**. *Joseph* **Ellison** vs *Thomas* **Parkham**.

Ordered that William **Irvine**, Haile **Talbot**, James **French** and Archibald **Woods** or any three be appointed to settle the administrator account of John **Glover**, administrator of Roland **Hoy**, deceased and make report.

A deed from Nicholas **Welch** and William **Buford** to Michael **Turney** proved by the oaths Joseph **Jack**, John **Carson** and John **Harris** and ordered recorded.

A deed from John **Biswell** to John **Carson** proved by John **Harris** and Joseph **Jack** and ordered certified.

A deed Thomas **Welch** to John **Giss** proved by Wiles **Cook**, John **Wilson** and Zachariah **Welch** and ordered recorded.

A power of attorney from Brightbury **Brow** to Robert **Rodes** proved by Higgason **Grubbs** and ordered recorded.

A deed from Richard **Cave** to Mary **Crawford** fully proved by the oath of Michael **Turner** and ordered recorded.

A deed from Michael **McNeely** to Ebenezor **Dickey** was acknowledged and ordered recorded.

A deed from Archibald **Woods** and *Mourning his wife* to Boud **Estill** was acknowledged and ordered recorded. femme relinquished.

A deed and Commission from William **Miller** and *Nancy his wife* to Michael **Wallace** fully proved by the oaths Robert **Dickey** and John **Manire** & ordered recorded.

The last will and testament of Joseph **McKinney** was proved by George **Adams** and John **Barrett** and ordered recorded. Probate is granted to James **Crawford** on the estate of Joseph **McKinney** whereupon he took the oath required by law and entered into bond conditioned as the Law directs. *Securities are Robert* **Henderson** *and William* **Miller**. Ordered that John

Province, George **Adams**, Alex **Denny** and James **Henderson** appraise the estate above.

Ordered that Michael **McNeely** be recommended to his Excellency as a proper person to be appointed as an Eschator.

On motion of William **Irvine**, Clerk of this Court, Isaac **Hockaday** is appointed his deputy whereupon he took the oath required by law.

William **McCulough** is exempted from paying County levy.

On the motion of William **West** his ear mark a crop a half pennny in the right out of the underside and a slit in the left.

William **Murray** vs *William* **Moore** judgment for £ 4-17-6 costs.

James **Greenlee** vs *William* **Nicholson** als. sum.

Thomas **Pasley** vs *Leonard* **Dozier** 42 shillings 6 pence and costs.

John **Leveridge** vs *Daniel* **Nichols** continued.

David **Southerland** vs *Benjamin* **Proctor** discontinued.

Deed from Leonard **Heatherly** to Henry **Noland** acknowledged and ordered recorded.

Deed from John **Hill** and *Elizabeth his wife* to William **Kerly** acknowledged. femme relinquished & ordered recorded.

Deed from James **French** to Lynch **Brooks** acknowledged and ordered recorded.

John **Tanner** vs *Higgason* **Grubbs** continued.

Same vs Same same.
Same vs Same same.
Same vs Same same.
Same vs Same same.
Same vs Same same.
Same vs Same same.
Same vs Same same.
Same vs Same same judgment for £ 2 and costs.
Same vs Same dismissed with costs.

Benjamin **Beall** asee vs *William* **Turpin** dismissed with costs.

Present James **French**, gent.

Deed from Alexander **Davis** and *Elizabeth his wife* to Henry **Noland** acknowledged. femme relinquished and ordered redorded.

Deed from same to Lynch **Brooks** same.

Madison County, Kentucky Court Order Book A

An account of John **Glover**, administrator of Roland **Hoy**, deceased was exhibited into Court and being previously passed by Commissioners for that purpose it was ordered to be recorded and he the said **Glover** is allowed the same out of the personal estate of the said deceased.

Andrew **McCalla** vs *John* **Harris** judgment for £ 1-10 and costs.
Humphrey **Best** vs *George* **James** continued.
James **Craig** vs *Henry* **Blair** als. sums.
Samuel **Estill** vs *Reuben* **Searcy** judgment for note and costs. £ *1-18-9.*
Jacob **Kimberlin** vs *Joel* **Short** judgment for note costs. £ *1-18-10.*
David **Noble** asee vs *Stephen* **White** continued.
Reuben **Smith** vs *Sherwood* **Harris** judgment £ 2-1 and costs.
Harris **Massie** vs *George* **Adams** motion continued.

A report of a road from near the mouth of Ravin Creek to intersect the Jacks Creek road near David **Crews** returned and established. Alex **Davis**, surveyor; Aaron **Lewis**, gent. to alott the tithes.

Joseph **Boutcher** appointed guardian to Joseph **Boutcher**, *Jr.* orphan of Joshua **Boutcher**, deceased whereupon he entered into bond conditioned.

Ordered that Robert **Rodes**, gent. alott the tithes to work under Jesse **Noland** surveyor of the road.

Ordered that Court adjourn until Court in Course.

Archibald **Woods**

At a Court held for Madison County on Tuesday the 2nd day of August 1791.

Present George **Adams**, James **Barnett**, Robert **Rodes** and John **Goggin**, gent.

Micheal **McNeely**, foreman; William **Calk**, John **Moore**, Joseph **Scott**, James **Martin**, George **Boone**, Baxlell **Maxwell**, Samuel **Boyd**, David **Gentry**, Samuel **Woods**, Thomas **Kennedy**, Charles **Ballew**, Benjamin **Oakley**, James **Boggs**, Alexander **Reed**, William **Robertson** and Joseph **Phelps** was sworn a Grand Jury for this County retired to consider of this presentments.

Francis **Cooper** discharged from payment of personal taxes and levies on account of his age and infirmity.

A deed from Lewis **Craig** to John **Yates** proved by John **Ilect** and Elijah **Hawkins** and ordered certified.

A deed from William **Bush** to David **Moore** was acknowledged and ordered recorded.

Ordered that the sheriff summons a jury and go on the lands of John **Moore** on the twentieth inst. and ascertain the damage that may be done by a road from opposite **Holder's** boatyard.

Ordered that Joseph **Woolfscale** be exempted from paying County levy.

Ordered that it be credited to the register of the Land Office that satisfactory proof was made to the Court that Elizabeth **Madden** is heir at law to George **Madden** and only surviving child.

Commonwealth vs *Solomon* **Asbell** judgment 5 shillings and costs.

Same vs *Walter* **Middleton** judgment 5 shillings and costs.

William **Harrison** vs *Zachariah* **Dozier** continued.

Robert **Adams** vs *Joseph* **Weldon** and wife continued.

Azariah **Martin** vs *John* **Bruce** continued.

Harris **Massie** vs *David* **Lynch** dismissed agreed.

Thomas **Kennedy** vs *Robert* **Dean** continued.

John **Holder** vs *William* **Hoys** executors continued.

James **Hagan** vs Same ditto.

James **Boggs** asee vs *John* **Holly** dismissed.

Nathan **Huston** vs *Zachariah* **Dozier** *In trespass, assault and battery* jury to inquire damage viz. David **Wells**, Asa **Searcy**, John **Nicheson**, Bathuel **Wrigs**, Andre **Huston**, Thomas **Maxwell**, William **Wallace**, John **Leveridge**, Samuel **Rice**, Barney **Stagner**, Alexander **Boyle**, Andrew **Kennedy** being sworn returned a verdict for plaintiff one penny damages and a new tryal at the defendants costs. *continued.*

Anthony **Rogers** vs *James* **Vaughn** dismissed.

Huston vs **Dozier** n. g. and Jd.

The Grand jury returned into Court and made the following presentments viz. the surveyor of the road down from Back Creek towards Danville to the County line for not keeping the same in repair.

The surveyor of the road from Robert **Henderson's** towards Lincoln Courthouse to the county line for not keeping the same in repair according to Law.

Also the surveyor of the road from Captain Archibald **Woods** to George **Boone** for not keeping the same in repair.

Also the surveyor of the road down Jacks Creek for not keeping the same in repair.

Also Jacob **Burgin** for swearing on the 13th day of July last at James **Martin** expressed in these words saying he would be God dammed.

The Commonwealth vs *James* **McCollister** information "A true bill".

The same vs *James* **Herrin** "not a true bill" for felony and the same is ordered to be summoned.

Zachariah **Dozier** to pay Hugh **Logan** 1 day and 60 miles against **Huston**.

Same to pay Mary **Huston** the same against the same.

Richard **Rannals** vs *Joseph* **Brown** continued.

John **South** vs *John* **Steal** continued.

Richard **Smith** on the demise of **Huston** vs *Henry* **Thompson**. Samuel **Morrow** tenant in possession admitted a defendant and confessed lease entry and ouster and pleads not guilty and stands on his title only and continued. *Samuel Morrow made a defendant in place of Henry Thompson in trespass and ejectment.*

William **Stewart** vs *Isaac* **Ingram**. Thomas **Batts** special bail writ inquiry set aside, nil debet & jd & continued for defendant. *Defendant does not owe debt.*

Fanny **Inglish** vs *Jesse* **May** writ inquiry set aside, not guilty & continued for plaintiff.

William **Irvine** administrator of Thomas **Reynolds** executed and acknowledged bond with Thomas **Todd** his security conditioned as the Law directs.

George **Boone**, James **Hockaday**, Isaac **Hockaday** and Richard **Callaway** are appointed to appraise the estate.

Zachariah **Dozier** to pay Isaac **Garvin** 1 day and traveling 36 miles vs **Huston**.

South vs **Hill** continued.

James **McNutt** vs *Robert* **Dean** jury to try issue viz. James **Barnett**, Thomas **Baker**, Peter **Taylor**, George **Wolfscale**, Samuel **Black**, Richard **Walker**, Evan **Watson**, Joshua **McQueen**, John **Carpenter**, John **Phelps**, Jeremiah **Perry** and Jesse **May** and returned verdict afterwards John **Phelps** with the consent of both parties was withdrawn and the cause continued.

Robert **Dean** to pay *Eusebrius* **Hubbard** for 5 days attendance vs *James* **McNutt**.

Robert **Dean** to pay Nicholas **Proctor** for 3 days attendance at the suit of *James* **McNutt**.

James **McNutt** to pay Richard **Estis** 1 days attendance against **Deane**.

Robert **Deane** to pay John **Gatridge** 2 days attendance against **Mitchell**.

John **Patten** vs *William* **Hicks** &c dedimus to take the deposition of William **Irvine**.

John **Weldon** vs *James* **Robinson** [*Robertson*] order reference set aside and the suit reinstated and remanded to the rule docket.

John **Blackburn** vs *John* **Johnson** writ inquiry set aside and payment & jd & continued.

Aaron **King** vs *Cornelius* **Dougherty** jury to inquire. Eusebries **Hubbard**, John **Adams**, William **Robertson**, Robert **Henry**, Robert **Knox**, William **Williams**, Asa **Searcy**, Francis **McNutt**, Samuel **Morrow**, Thomas **Bergin**, Moore **Kincaid** and John **Sappington** and returned verdict for the plaintiff the debt in the dicts mentioned and one penny for the damages & judgment. £ 8-10 *damages*.

James **Craig** vs *Henry* **Blair** judgment for £ 4 and costs.

Ordered that James **McNutt** be fined five pounds for fighting and insulting the Court.

Also Robert **Deane** three pounds for the same.

Ordered that Court adjourn until tomorrow 9 oclock.

George **Adams**

At a Court continued and held for Madison County on Wednesday the 3rd day of August 1791.

Present George **Adams**, James **Barnett**, Aaron **Lewis**, Robert **Rodes**, James **French** and John **Goggins**.

James **Burton** vs *Drury* **Willis** dismissed at defendant costs.

Mack **Neely** *Michael McNeely* vs *John* **Adams** continued.

James **Stephenson** vs *William* **Robertson** continued for plaintiff.

James **Stephenson** to pay Mary **Gass** 2 days attendance vs *William* **Robinson** [*Robertson*].

Madison County, Kentucky Court Order Book A   131

Richard **Dunn** vs *Christopher* **Irvine's** heir *David Irvine*, ordered that James **French**, John **Miller**, John **Woods** and Robert **Rodes**, gent. or any three do view the said tracts of land and lay of to the said complaintant 100 acres in such manner as will do equal right and justice to the parties and report their proceedings to February Court next and that the surveyor attend and lay of the same.

John **Tanner** vs *Higgason* **Grubbs** Issue waived and judgment by non sum. £ 14.

John **Tanner** vs *Higgason* **Grubbs** Jury to try issue viz. Yelverton **Peyton**, Samuel **Estill**, Andrew **Bogie**, William **Coughran**, Matthew **Scott**, Francis **McNutt**, John **Boggs**, John **Nicholson**, James **McNutt**, William **Wallace**, Richard **Gorden** and Robert **Yancy** and returned verdict for plaintiff £ 22-10 damages.

Aaron **Lewis** vs *Boud* **Estill** Jury to try issue towit. Stephen **Hancock**, Asa **Searcy**, Robert **Harris**, William **Miller**, Payton **Robinson**, Nicholas **Hawkins**, Higgason **Grubbs**, Andrew **Huston**, William **Kerley**, Anthony **Rogers**, William **Woolfscale**, James **Stephenson** returned verdict for plaintiff £ 6-2-6 damages.

Joseph **Scott** vs *Thomas* **Boyer** continued.

Humphrey **Best** vs *James* **Mason** continued for plaintiff.

Matthew **Patterson** vs *Robert* **Dean** continued and dedimus to take the deposition of Andrew **Wiley** and Samuel **Ewing**.

Charles **Boyd** vs *Thomas* **Batts** Jury to Inquire of damages towit. Andrew **Bogie**, William **Wallace**, Samuel **Estill**, John **Boggs**, John **Nicholson**, Richard **Gorden**, Robert **Yance**, Francis **McNutt**, Yelverton **Peyton**, Matthew **Scott**, James **McNutt**, William **Cochran** returned verdict for plaintiff. £ 12 and costs.

Jonathan **Owsley** vs *James* **Shackelford** dismissed.

Charles **Boyd** to pay Thomas **Owsley** 3 days attendance vs *Thomas* **Batts**.

John **Leveridge** vs *Daniel* **Nicols** continued.

Thomas **Batts** to pay William **Boyd** 3 days attendance against *Charles* **Boyd**.

Charles **Boyd** to pay Hardy **Rolls** one day and 36 miles vs *Thomas* **Batts**.

Same to pay James **Coghill** one day and forty two miles.

John **Roberts** vs *John* **Bradley** dismissed.
Humphrey **Best** vs *George* **James** dismissed at plaintiff costs.
John **Leveridge** to pay George **Christal** 2 days attendance and 27 miles vs **Nicholson**.
David **Noble** vs *Stephen* **White** dismissed agreed.
John **Adams** assee vs *Dodson* **Thorp** als.
Aaron **Lewis** to pay John **South** two days vs *Boud* **Estill**.
Same to pay William **South** vs the same.
Humphrey **Best** to pay William **Miller** two days vs *George* **James**.
James to pay John **King** to days attendance in the suit of *Humphrey* **Best** the same to pay Emanuel **Celly** for two day attendance in the suit of the same.
Andrew **Bogie** vs *Higgason* **Grubbs** dismissed at plaintiff.
John **Tanner** vs *Higgason* **Grubbs** judgment. £ 4.
Same vs Same Same(repeated 6 times).
Edward **Turner** vs *David* **Massey** continued.
Commonwealth vs *James* **McNutt** the fine suspended until further order of the Court.
Same vs *Robert* **Dean** same order.
Ordered that John **Collier** prepare a sufficient house for transfer tobacco against the fifteenth of October next.
Ordered that Court adjourn until Court in Course.

George **Adams**

Glossary

ABATES: to put an end to. A case is ended due to the death of one of the parties or removal of one of the parties to another jurisdiction.

ALS SUMS: defendant is summoned to appear at court.

ASSEE: abbreviation for assignee; the person to whom an assignment is made.

DE BENE ESSE: used in relation to a dedimus. A witness is examined in anticipation of a future need. Their testimony is important and they may be unavailable at the time it is needed.

DEDIMUS: court order allowing a deposition to be taken for a witness who cannot appear in court in person.

DEFENDANT: the person or persons against whom a complaint is brought.

DEPOSITION: written testimony of a witness who cannot appear in court.

FEME RELINQUISHED: wife relinquished her dower right in the property being sold.

JOINT TENANTS: property is held by two or more persons for life or at will with one deed or title.

PLAINTIFF: the person who files a complaint against another person.

PROTEMPORE: temporary.

RECOGNIZANCE: an obligation to appear in court on a certain day.

REPLEVY BOND: a bond for the recovery of goods claimed to have been wrongfully taken or detained, upon the person giving security to try the matter in Court and return the goods if defeated.

TENANTS IN COMMON: property is held by two or more persons each with a distinct title.

TITHE: a tax or the person being taxed. Traditionally this tax is 10% of the persons income, but in this book the tax is a fixed rate for each adult male.

VESTED: rights are fixed, absolute, complete.

WRIT OF AD QUOD DAMNUM: an order of the court commanding the sheriff to make inquiry into damage that will be done by a certain act. Also used to condemn land for public use such as a road.

WRIT OF INQUIRY: issued after the plaintiff has obtained a judgment by default, directing the sheriff and jury to inquire into the amount of plaintiff demands and assess damages.

Index

A

ABNER: Joshua, 10, 13, 122
ADAMS: Aggnes, 87; Fothergil, 79, 110; George, 1, 5, 7, 9, 10, 14, 16, 21-23, 29-32, 34, 39, 47-49, 51, 53, 56, 63, 66, 68, 69, 75, 77, 81, 83-85, 87, 88, 90, 94, 97, 102, 105, 106, 113, 125-127; George Jr., 64; Hanah, 20; James, 3, 5, 20, 30, 39, 46, 53, 87, 102; John, 12, 30, 34, 44, 48, 49, 54, 55, 58, 60, 62, 64, 68, 71, 72, 76, 82, 83, 102, 113, 130, 132; Mathew, 32, 61, 102, 120; Robert, 20, 71, 74, 90, 97, 107, 114, 119, 128; William, 46
ADDISON: William, 91
AHERN: Edward, 80
ALCORN: James, 63; John, 63, 101
ALLEGREE: Mathew, 100
ALLEN: Gary, 105; James, 86; John, 17; William, 70
AMDAM: Hanah, 20
AMHERST COUNTY, 69
AMOCKS: Matthew, 43; Samuel, 43
ANDERSON: Isaac, 16, 21, 24, 61, 81; James, 3, 10, 12, 21, 22, 62, 66, 71, 72, 75, 88, 118, 122; Jasa, 61; John, 2, 5, 11, 16, 22, 26, 31, 36, 41, 46, 49, 55, 56, 58, 59, 64, 65, 68, 71, 80, 95, 104, 109, 112; Samuel, 116; William, 16, 24, 44, 51, 60, 61, 102
ANSON COUNTY, NC, 71
ANTROBUS: William, 110
ARMSTRONG: John, 90
ARNOLD: Humphrey, 45
ARTHER: Talbot, 11, 14
ASBELL: Solomon, 118, 128
ATTORNIES, 14, 35, 41, 47, 62, 86, 105, 118

B

BAILEY: John, 104
BAISLEY/BAZELY: James, 17; John, 19
BAKER: Thomas, 40, 44, 70, 76, 81, 82, 88, 129
BALLEW/BALLOU: Charles, 17, 42, 65, 121, 127
BANKS, 27, 57, 115: Andrew, 106, 112; Thomas, 14, 16, 17, 56, 60, 70, 119
BARDGES: William, 109
BARKSHIRE: Dukrey, 38
BARNETT: Alexander, 89; George, 27; James, 1, 8, 10, 12, 13, 18, 25, 29, 30, 33, 35, 57, 62, 66, 67, 69, 70, 72, 75, 80, 83, 84, 88, 89, 91, 93, 94, 100, 102, 107, 112, 120, 129; John, 69, 81, 89, 97, 107, 113, 125; Joseph, 93; William, 54, 66, 83, 113
BARROW: Richard, 5, 116
BARTLET: William, 2, 9, 77
BARTON: Abraham, 21; Joshua, 55; Robert, 55, 92; Samuel, 122; Thomas, 20
BATTS: Thomas, 89, 90, 92, 97, 106, 113, 114, 119, 129, 131
BATY: Daniel, 45
BAUGH: Joseph, 102

Index

BEALL: Andrew, 18, 19; Benjamin, 126; Walter, 18, 19, 111
BELL: Archibald, 12, 60, 63
BENNETT: Hardy, 67, 124
BENTON: Robert, 48
BERRY/BARRY: James, 2, 6, 43, 44, 113, 119
BEST, 67: Humphrey, 3, 11, 16, 19, 22, 31, 36, 41, 44, 46, 48, 55, 65, 69, 72, 73, 75, 77, 78, 82, 86, 89, 98, 101, 106, 107, 109, 114, 127, 131, 132; Phebe, 74; Stephen, 82, 109
BIGGERSTAFF/BICKERSTAFF, 107: Samuel, 75, 80, 85, 87, 96, 103, 105-107, 113
BISWELL: John, 34, 125
BLACK: Andrew, 108; Ellender, 83; James, 22, 24, 26, 33, 48, 50, 67, 83, 92, 100, 104, 117; John, 44, 61, 78, 80, 83, 106, 114, 115, 121; Samuel, 78, 114, 129; Thomas, 108, 121
BLACKBURN: John, 130
BLAIR: Henry, 127, 130
BLAND: Charles, 121
BLEDSOE: Joseph, 102, 104; William, 64
BLITHE: William, 96
BLOCKLEY: James, 92; John, 85, 87
BOGGS: James, 96, 108, 109, 113-115, 119, 127, 128; John, 131
BOGIE/BOGEY: Andrew, 13, 16, 112, 113, 117, 121; Andrew, Jr., 121; Andrew, 131-2; James, 121

BOLCH: John, 60
BOONE/BOON: Ann, 91; Daniel, 45, 108; George, 4, 6, 31, 74, 76, 91, 104, 127-129; Josiah, 98; Lydia, 15; Squire, 83, 86, 97, 98
BOONSBOROUGH: election at, 62, 78, 93; plan of, 102; store at, 37
BOUTCHER: Joseph, 127; Joseph, Jr., 127; Joshua, 127
BOWERS: Ann, 60
BOWMAN: William, 36
BOYD: Abraham, 66, 68; Charles, 97, 106, 113, 119, 131; George, 90, 106, 114; Jane, 78; Samuel, 66, 78, 79, 83, 88, 100, 104, 113, 127; William, 131
BOYER/BOWYER: Henry, 80; Thomas, 30, 84, 131
BOYLES: Alexander, 85, 116, 128; John, 1, 3, 5, 7, 10, 17, 20, 25, 34, 53, 63, 69, 72, 75, 76, 78, 83
BRADEN: Robert, 106, 107
BRADLEY: John, 132; Thomas, 75
BRAMWELL: Joseph, 115; Richard, 77
BRANKS: Jane, 102; Robert, 2, 28, 44, 77, 102, 112; Robert, Sr., 18;
BRATTON: John, 84, 86
BRENT: John, 121
BRIDGES: William, 93, 109
BRINSON: Stout, 65
BRISCOE: William, 20, 22, 43, 86, 112
BROCKMAN: Thomas, 94
BROOKS, 49: Ebenezer, 119; Elisha, 80-82, 86, 87, 109, 110,

BROOKS (cont.): 120, 122; Lynch, 126; Robert, 41, 49, 56, 87
BROUGHTON: John, 86
BROW: Brightbury, 125
BROWN: Absolom, 8; Benjamin, 27, 44, 49, 56, 65; James, 35, 82; John, 63, 72, 79, 80, 96; Joseph, 58, 79, 80, 87, 96, 129; Rabbi, 34; Richard, 115; Samuel, 81, 82, 86, 88, 107, 109; Stephen, 109; Thomas, 23, 25, 32; William, 89
BROWNFIELD: Robert, 48
BRUCE/BRUSE: John, 41, 46, 55, 82, 87, 89, 90, 97, 105, 107, 113, 119, 128
BRUNDAEG/BRUNDIGE: Solomon, 12, 18, 19
BRYANT: James, 108; John, 76, 110
BUFORD: Abraham, 53, 70, 93; William, 125
BULLOCK: David, 116, 120; Len Henly, 29
BURGIN/BERGEN: Dennis, 9, 42; Isaac, 68, 109, 116; Jacob, 56, 72, 80, 87, 129; Thomas, 130
BURNETT: Margaret, 84; Rowland, 84, 98
BURNSIDES: James, 89
BURRASS: Charles, 100
BURTON/BARTON: Abraham, 21, 26, 75, 80, 89, 92, 114; Allen, 26, 64, 88, 93, 95-97, 101, 111, 114-116; Isaac, 35, 50, 90; James, 130; Jane, 50, 94; Jane Sr., 95; John, 21; Joshua, 55; Rachel, 50; Robert, 26, 44, 55, 58, 60, 64, 76, 80, 81, 92, 96, 97, 101; Samuel, 113, 122; Sarah, 35; Thomas, 20
BUSH: Philip, 12, 15; William, 75, 80, 89, 96, 105, 128
BUTCHER: Joseph, 42, 43, 52, 54, 66; William, 43, 58, 91, 106
BUTLER: John, 48, 49; Philip, 56; Thomas, 49, 56, 68

C

CABELL: William, Sr., 69
CALDWELL: William, 90, 107
CALK: William, 12, 13, 27, 34, 43-45, 48, 84, 104, 117, 119, 127
CALLAWAY: Caleb, 32, 109, 110; Doshia, 32; Elizabeth, 45; Flanders, 12, 43, 56, 65, 108; James, 49, 56; John, 32; Richard, 32, 45, 61, 92, 129; William, 56, 65
CAMPBELL, 82: Charles, 8, 69, 72, 75, 78, 82, 86, 98, 101, 106, 107, 109, 114; Hugh, 9, 15, 17, 20, 28, 36, 43, 44, 46, 96, 112; James, 8; John, 15, 19, 32, 67, 70, 91; Samuel, 13, 88; Thomas, 25, 43, 49, 50, 67, 70
CARPENTER: John, 10, 26, 38, 88, 92, 113, 129
CARR: William, 84
CARSON: John, 121, 125
CARTRIGHT: Jesse, 45, 46; Jestinean, 46
CAVE: Elizabeth, 121; Richard, 121, 125
CELLY: Emanuel, 132

CHALFREY/CHAFRAY, 48: Charles, 5, 14, 32, 42, 44
CHENAULT/SHINNALL: William, 48, 59, 76, 81, 84
CHILES: John, 43; Thomas, 71
CHINN, 41, 49, 58, 64, 68, 71: Christopher, 37; Thomas, 90
CLARK: Baptist, 17, 19, 23, 25, 27, 41, 43, 44, 48, 49, 56, 57, 61-63, 65; Bennett, 121; Edward, 49; Godfrey, 83; James, 36, 83; John, 17, 27, 36, 68, 83, 87, 93, 106, 110; Margaret, 83; Robert, Jr., 121; Robert, Sr., 121; William, 83
CLAY: Green, 3, 4, 8, 11, 16, 23, 33, 35, 38, 45, 48, 55, 56, 58, 60, 62, 64, 66, 68, 71, 73, 79, 83, 88, 92, 93, 99, 103-105, 112, 121
CLEVELAND: Eli, 17
CLINE: John, 12, 17, 19, 23, 41, 49, 58, 68, 71, 75
CLINTON: Archibald, 20
COBURN, 89
COCHRAN/COUGHRAN: Dennis, 68; John, 66, 71, 72, 81, 85, 96; Samuel, 44, 59, 60, 66, 80, 85, 94, 96, 100, 108; William, 113, 131
COFER: Jesse, 70, 92
COFFE: Ambrose, 2
COGHILL: James, 106, 131
COLEFOOT: John, 77
COLLIER: John, 39, 41, 45, 46, 63, 70, 80, 81, 88, 99, 132
COLSON: John, 98, 105

CONRAD: Nicholas, 115
COOK: David, 102; Wiles, 125; Wilis, 87
COOLEY: William, 110
COOMLEY: David, 40
COOPER: Benjamin, 44, 61, 65, 80, 88, 117; Bracton, 109; Francis, 127; Sarshall/Sarshwell, 65, 81, 89, 106, 107, 109
CORTNEY/COURTNEY: John, 12, 18, 69, 72, 75, 81
COSGROVE: James, 25, 64
COUNTY LEVY: 1787, 28; 1788, 50; 1789, 77; 1790, 108
COURBOURN: John, 41
COURTHOUSE: at the Gass house, 5; building of, 9, 30; plans for, 30, 33; sale of temporary, 47; store at, 58; temporary, 10
COWAN: James, 58
COWHERT: James, 125
CRAFT: William, 95
CRAIG: James, 127, 130; Joseph, 83, 102; Lewis, 127
CRAMPTON/COMPTON: Hezekiah, 73, 75, 80, 82, 87
CRAWFORD/CRAFFORD: James, 11, 16, 22, 26, 31, 41, 43, 46, 55, 65, 67; Mary, 37, 121, 125; Rebeckah, 41; William, 22, 124
CREATH: William, 95, 106, 113-115, 118, 119, 122
CREWS/CRUSE: Andrew, 96; David, 5, 7, 12, 13, 30, 31, 39, 42, 43, 46, 49, 54, 59, 73, 94, 99, 100, 102, 109, 110, 122, 127;

CREWS (cont.): Elijah, 12; Jeremiah, 13, 73, 118; Thomas, 28, 30, 47, 59, 109
CROOK: Absolom, 16-18, 42, 125; John, 116
CROW: John, 83, 86, 97, 98
CRYSTAL/CHRISTAL: George, 132

D

DAMON: Samuel, 55
DANIEL: Martin, 110; Robert, 110; Thomas, 44
DANIELS: Walker, 44, 48
DAUGHERTY: Cornelius, 23-25, 29, 37, 46, 48, 71, 73, 99, 106, 107, 114, 116, 130; Cornlius, 31; Isabel, 23, 25, 29; Margaret, 99
DAVIDSON: George, 71
DAVIS: Alexander, 57, 58, 102, 126, 127; Elizabeth, 126; James, 5, 23; Jane, 61, 74; John, 38, 86, 112; Prudence, 107; Richard, 55; Samuel, 8, 27, 38, 61, 74, 78; Thomas, 118; Zachariah, 122
DAWSON: Bartholomew, 56, 63; Samuel, 63; Thomas, 63
DEAN/DEANE: Robert, 44, 58, 69, 90, 91, 97, 99, 106, 11-2, 114-5, 119, 120, 128-132
DEBRIELL/DIBRELL: Charles, 15, 19, 38, 51, 54, 58, 64, 66, 68, 80, 88, 90, 97, 101, 111, 115, 116
DEDMAN: Samuel, 119
DENHAM/DUNHAM: William, 46, 79
DENNY: Alexander, 3, 20, 25, 35, 102, 108, 126
DEVER/DIVER/DOVER: Dennis, 53, 62, 64, 68, 76, 77, 102; John, 96
DEWES: Lewis, 48
DICKEY: Ebenezer, 125; Robert, 125
DODS: Andrew, 66
DONALSON: Andrew, 67, 68, 81, 89, 97, 106, 107, 113
DOOLEY/DOLEY/DOLLY: Jacob, 94; M., 70; Moses, 10, 14, 16, 20, 27, 36, 39, 57, 61, 63, 73, 86, 92, 116-7
DOTY: John, 4, 10, 17, 27, 101
DOZIER/DOZER: James, 23, 57, 58, 64; James I., 27, 45, 58, 66-68, 102, 118, 122; John, 90, 101, 103; Leonard, 100, 115, 118, 126; Zachariah, 11, 15, 16, 18, 19, 22, 26, 27, 36, 42, 43, 46, 49, 54, 57, 64, 67, 68, 73, 79, 80, 86, 87, 90, 96-98, 104, 106, 107, 113-116, 119, 120, 128, 129
DRYDEN: Mary, 71, 116; William, 26, 37, 64, 68, 71, 75, 82, 116, 122
DUGLAS: Alexander, 70
DUNCAN: Benjamin, 78, 113-115, 122; Samuel, 55
DUNN: Richard, 131
DURBIN: Edward, 38, 102; Joseph, 38
DURHAM: James, 35
DYER: John, 17, 66; Mary, 104

E

EAST: North, 121
EASTIN: Richard, 27
EDWARDS: Uriah, 30, 44, 49, 60
ELLIOTT: George, 73
ELLIS: John, 25
ELLISON: Joseph, 122, 125; Richard, 91
EMBRY: Jesse, 70, 74, 76, 99, 103, 121; Joel, 95, 122; John, 94
EMMERSON: Jesse, 64
ENGLAND: David, 94, 103, 112
ENGLISH: Fanny, 114, 129
ESTILL: Benjamin, 33, 44; Boud, 11, 16, 20-22, 26, 27, 36, 37, 41, 46, 50, 77, 99, 100, 119, 125, 131, 132; Captain, 7, 19; James, 33, 44, 49, 57, 102; John, 121; Jonathan, 33; Samuel, 2, 4, 21, 22, 24, 26, 30, 32, 33, 43, 49, 55, 59, 61, 62, 67, 69, 74, 77, 102, 112, 116, 118, 123, 124, 127, 131; Sarrah, 33; Wallace, 33, 53, 59, 77; William, 118, 124
ESTILL'S STATION, 26, 29, 36
ESTIS: Gehue, 114; George, 114; Reubin, 114; Richard, 114, 130
EVANS: Peter, 43, 49, 57, 66, 84, 85, 92, 105, 112, 117, 118
EWING: Samuel, 66, 131

F

FARRIS/FARIS, 86, 87: Micajah, 74, 100; Michael, 27, 54, 81, 100, 114, 115; Moses, 58, 59, 80, 106, 107; Thomas, 35, 80, 83
FARWELL: John, 110
FEAR: Edward, 49, 56, 65
FENNELL/FINNELL: James, 24, 67, 104; William, 24, 56
FENTON, 49: Bartholomew, 35, 37, 42, 57, 65
FERRY: at Paint Lick, 53; at Sugar Creek, 56; Boonsborough, 32, 33; Tates Creek, 92; Turpen's, 40
FIELDS: Henry, 109, 116
FINLEY/FENLEY: David, 61; George, 61, 65, 106
FINNEY: James, 36; Wm, 44
FITZGERALD/FITZGERRALL/FITZJOREL, 68: John, 58, 72, 98, 107
FLEMING: Robert, 122
FOWLER: Matthew, 91; Richard, 38
FRANCES/FRANCIS: John, 55, 61
FREEMAN: Samuel, 14, 41, 73, 79, 96, 104
FRENCH: Cuzza, 32; Giles, 67; Henry, 43; James, 3, 6, 7, 10, 12, 13, 16, 18, 21, 24, 27, 33, 34, 44, 45, 48, 51, 52, 58, 59, 62, 64-69, 72, 74, 75, 78, 82, 93, 101, 110, 124-126, 131; John, 51
FUGET/FUGIT: Thomas, 80, 87

G

GADDY: Elijah, 69
GALLAHAR/GALLIHER: Patrick, 24, 67, 68, 90, 97, 107
GALLISPIE: William, 88, 97
GARVIN: Isaac, 106, 115
GASS: David, 1, 4, 5, 7, 8, 10, 20, 22, 25, 31, 33, 40, 46, 50, 62, 69, 83, 84, 91, 100, 109, 112, 113; John, 16, 24, 33, 60, 77, 109,

GASS (cont.): 112, 122, 125; Mary, 130; Thomas, 5, 33, 37, 42
GATER: Peter, 60
GATLIN: William, 58, 64, 68
GATRIDGE: John, 130
GENTRY: David, 58, 74, 108, 112; David, Sr., 118; David, 118, 119, 122, 127; Reubin, 94; Richard, 74, 79, 119; Simon, 75, 80
GEORGE: George, 99; Mary Ann, 99; Nicholas, 1, 4; Whison, 67
GILLETT/GILLIT: Jonathan, 105, 111, 116, 118
GIST/GEST/GUIST: Thomas, 41, 59, 63, 81, 88, 89
GIVEN: Samuel, 101
GLENN: William, 18
GLOVER: John, 109, 111, 125, 127
GOGGIN/GOGGINS: John, 30, 61, 62, 75, 80, 101, 111
GOODLOE: William, 109, 118
GORDEN/GORDON, 41, 89: John, 17, 19; Richard, 55, 58, 72, 102, 131; Samuel, 4, 34, 36, 37, 41, 60, 65, 73
GRAHAM: Flanagan, 111; Mary, 118
GRASON: Benjamin, 23
GRAY/GREY, 49: George, 37, 44, 49, 56, 65
GREENLEE: James, 120, 126
GREENUP: Christopher, 41, 82
GRIFFIN: William, 23
GRUBBS: Captain, 8, 19; Higgason, 2, 4, 14, 15, 27, 28, 30, 42, 46, 49, 55, 58, 59, 62, 68, 72, 74, 91, 94-96, 98, 101, 115, 119, 125, 126, 131, 132; Lucy, 14, 27, 46, 62, 91
GUINN/GWINN: Mathew, 58;
GULLEY: Thomas, 93, 95
GUNNEL: John, 48

H

HACKETT: Peter, 26, 44, 59, 68
HADEN: Samuel, 53
HALL: David, 70, 76, 83, 105, 122; Edward, 43; Moses, 43; Thomas, 14, 28, 73, 77, 84
HALLEY/HOLLEY/HOLLY: Francis, 22, 39, 92; John, 10, 16, 22, 37, 38, 43, 46, 51, 61, 73, 75, 80, 89, 96, 97, 105, 113, 128
HAM: Joseph, 119; William, 2, 4, 8, 16, 17, 19, 72, 78, 90-93, 114
HAM'S MILL, 55
HANCOCK/HANDCOCK: Joseph, 59; Kitty, 57; Stephen, 9, 11, 16, 22, 24, 36, 40, 57, 58, 60, 65, 79, 88, 96, 131; William, 11, 15, 16, 22, 27, 31, 36, 41, 64-66, 73, 86, 112
HARDAGE: William, 98
HARDWICK: John, 21
HARE: Andrew, 64, 68, 71, 73, 86, 89, 90, 98, 111
HARMON: Israel, 64, 68, 69, 71, 72, 75, 81
HARPER: John, 67
HARRIS, 41: Andrew, 65, 70, 80, 89, 112; Christopher, 38, 41, 47, 50, 53, 58, 59, 109; James, 38, 80, 82; John, 23, 55, 60, 72, 120,

HARRIS (cont.): 125, 127; Nancy, 64; Robert, 64, 131; Samuel, 23, 34, 53, 113; Sherwood, 29, 88, 125, 127; Thomas, 34, 36, 55, 56; Thomson, 36, 37; William, 64, 68, 71, 73, 89, 98, 111

HARRISON: William, 80, 90, 97, 106, 113, 119, 128

HARRODSBURG: trustees of, 54, 58, 64, 75, 81, 114

HART: George, 71; Thomas, 57, 110

HARVEY: William, 81

HAW: James, 7

HAWKINS: Elijah, 127; Joseph, 114; Nathan, 95, 96; Nicholas, 27, 34, 38, 55, 66, 75, 80, 84, 90, 109, 113, 131

HAYS: Susannah, 61, 73; William, 61, 73

HEATH: Andrew, 27

HEATHERLY/HETHERLY: Leon, 73; Leonard, 19, 65, 79, 104, 126

HELTON/HILTON/HOLTON: Jesse, 54, 57; John, 54, 57, 66, 74, 82, 89

HENDERSON, 66, 77: Archibald, 55, 60; Elizabeth, 60; Frances, 98, 99; Franky, 72; James, 25, 63, 65, 72, 77, 126; Joseph, 116; Michael, 94; Pleasant, 55, 60; Richard, 55, 60, 109; Robert, 11, 22, 23, 25, 27, 31, 36, 41, 46, 47, 65, 67, 68, 70, 72, 73, 77, 94, 98, 99, 101, 102, 125, 128

HENDRICKS/HENDRIX: James, 5, 7, 15, 31, 37, 58, 71, 75, 89, 91, 100, 117

HENRY: Robert, 42, 65, 67, 83, 130; William, 54

HERRIN: James, 123, 129

HERRING: Edmund, 48

HIATT: Ame, 78; John, 63

HICKMAN, 86: Lydia, 82, 107; Richard, 82, 106, 107, 112, 122

HICKS/HIX: Daniel, 71, 86, 103; John, 119; William, 96, 108, 109, 111, 115, 130

HIGGENSON: Thomas, 71

HILL, 129: Clement, 110; Elizabeth, 126; James, 113; Joel, 45, 65, 87, 122; John, 74, 126; Robert, 23, 27

HINDS: James, 42

HINTON: George, 53, 93, 112

HISLE: John, 60

HOCKADAY: Edmund, 98, 106, 112; Isaac, 126, 129; James, 129; John, 98

HODGES, 49: Jesse, 2, 8, 17, 27, 48, 49, 67, 68, 109, 112

HODGE'S SETTLEMENT, 94

HOGAN/HOGEN: David, 12, 17, 28, 63; Elizabeth, 63; James, 58, 71, 75, 82, 89, 98, 105, 128; Philip, 38

HOLDER, 84: Fanny, 32; Frances, 100; John, 11, 14, 54, 66, 75, 80, 89, 98, 100, 117, 122, 128; William, 105

HOLEMAN: John, 88

HOLLAND/HOLLAN, 64: William, 2, 4, 44, 48, 55, 58, 60, 68, 73, 82, 85, 86, 93, 98, 99, 103
HOPKINS: John, 54, 67, 68, 90, 103, 112; William, 14
HOPPER: John, 105; Samuel, 75, 80, 87, 96, 105-107, 113; Thomas, 122; William, 68, 75, 113
HORN: Christopher, 49, 94; Joseph, 77, 99
HOWARD: James, 43, 65, 67, 88; William, 58
HOWS: William, 70
HOY: John, 105; Patsey, 109; Roland, 94, 109, 125, 127; Sarah, 17, 19, 70, 71, 73, 116; William, 14, 16-20, 42, 48, 64, 66, 69-73, 75, 80, 82, 85-87, 89, 94, 98, 99, 111, 114, 116, 128
HUBBARD: Eusebrius, 114, 130
HUCHERSON: Charles, 62
HUGHBANK: Achilles, 67
HUGHS: Absolem, 59
HUGVET: Thomas, 21
HUME: Gerrard, 2
HUNT: Basil, 111; John, 96, 109, 111, 114, 115, 118; William, 119
HUNTER: John, 73
HUSTON: Andrew, 93, 128, 131; Jesse, 93, 121; John, 99; Mary, 106, 115, 129; Nathan, 98, 106, 107, 114, 116, 119, 120, 128

I
ILECT: John, 127
INGRAM: Isaac, 112, 129

INNES: Harry, 1, 66, 68, 81, 86, 115
IRVINE: Christopher, 1, 6, 78, 82, 107, 122, 131; David, 78, 131; Francis, 78; Lydia, 6, 17, 32, 107; Molly, 78; Samuel, 86; William, 1, 6, 17, 24, 33, 45, 46, 50, 51, 61, 69, 70, 77-79, 84, 92, 94, 98, 103, 112, 116, 118, 125, 126, 129, 130
IRWIN: Samuel, 96

J
JACK: Joseph, 125
JACKSON: Elizabeth, 73; Isaiah, 86; John, 56, 64, 73, 76, 104, 117
JACOBS: Thomas, 112, 119
JAIL: insuffiency of, 51
JAMES: Daniel, 47; George, 127, 132; Tobias, 112
JAMESON: Samuel, 41, 91
JETT: Stephen, 103
JOHNSON: Andrew, 68; Benjamin, 65, 66; James, 54, 91, 118; John, 49, 130
JONES, 86: Cadd, 103; Charles, 56; Irvin, 110; Irvine, 70, 71; John, 72, 76, 82, 84; Mary, 71, 122; Nicholas, 60; Thomas, 91, 121; William, 30, 39, 46, 71, 73, 79, 85, 93, 94, 109, 115, 116, 118, 119, 122

K
KAID: John, 108
KAVANAUGH/CAVANAUGH: Ann, 24; Captain, 7, 19; Charles,

KAVANAUGH (cont.): 2, 6, 9, 15, 35, 66, 74, 101; Charles Jr., 9; Charles Sr., 38, 39, 59; Phileman, 24, 26, 38; William, 24, 35, 59, 103, 105, 122

KENDY: Joseph, 61

KENNEDY, 67, 89: Agnes, 117, 121; Andrew, 11, 16, 18-9, 22, 26-9, 31, 46, 48, 55, 65, 73, 79, 86, 102, 106, 112, 115, 118, 128; Captain, 7, 19; David, 66, 75, 93; James, 76; Jeremiah, 96; John, 31, 46, 83, 89, 91, 96; Joseph, 1, 2, 5, 6, 19, 21, 27, 31-3, 36, 43-4, 51, 53, 61, 63, 69-70, 75, 82, 84, 112; Patsy, 70; Thomas, 1, 3, 8, 10-1, 13, 15-6, 20, 22, 29, 36, 41, 43-4, 46-8, 53, 55-7, 62-3, 65-6, 68, 70, 72-3, 75, 77, 80-2, 88-90, 96-7, 99, 102, 104, 106, 112-4, 117-9, 121, 127, 128

KENNEY/CANNEY: Alexander, 58, 43, 66

KERLEY/KERLY/KERTLEY: Elijah, 125; John, 105, 125; William, 43, 44, 82, 88, 90, 98, 114, 115, 125, 126, 131

KILPATRICK: Hugh, 47, 57, 72; Robert, 36, 66, 79, 86

KIMBERLAN/KIMBERLIN: Abraham, 124; Jacob, 127

KINCAID, 59: David, 91; John, 17, 41, 43, 48, 58, 59, 62, 66, 67, 73, 86, 96, 104, 112; John Jr., 85, 91, 100, 103; Moore, 130; Robert, 32, 61, 75, 93, 124; William, 67, 68, 123, 124

KING, 49, 115: Aaron, 25, 26, 32, 42, 57, 66, 73, 75, 80, 82, 87, 101, 104, 119, 130; Hannah, 101; John, 132

KIRKPATRICK: Robert, 43, 104

KNAVE: Robert, 115

KNOX, 68: James, 34, 121; John, 93, 108; Robert, 93, 114, 121, 130; Thomas, 72

L

LACKEY: Thomas, 83

LAND: Thomas, 122

LANE: John, 23

LAUGHLIN: Henry, 117

LAWRENCE: Thomas, 102

LEAVINGSTON: Thomas, 23

LEITCH: Henry, 58

LEVERAGE/LEVERIDGE: John, 24, 83, 92, 120, 126, 128, 131, 132

LEWIS: Aaron, 5, 10, 20, 21, 27, 31, 38, 45, 47, 52, 60, 76, 80, 88, 92, 94, 98, 99, 103, 108, 109, 116, 118, 119, 127, 131, 132; Jacob, 88; John, 42, 110; Thomas, 27, 85, 110, 122

LIQUOR: price of, 12, 51, 57, 97, 120

LOCKHART/LOCKHEART/LOCKART, 64: Patrick, 43, 49, 57, 68, 71

LOGAN: Hugh, 106, 120, 129; John, 1, 11; Matthew, 111; Nathaniel, 35, 37; Thimothy, 16, 22, 41, 46, 55

LOGSDON: Edward, 70; Joe, 104; Joseph, 46; Mary, 70
LONG: Elizabeth, 49
LONGSTRETH: Jonathan, 12, 41, 54, 87, 89
LOWRY: James, 90
LUTTERELL: John, 122
LYNCH: David, 11, 43, 44, 49, 50, 58, 62, 67, 82, 87, 89, 107, 115, 128

M

MCALLISTER/MCCOLLISTER: James, 89, 93, 106, 117, 118, 120, 129; John, 102; William, 101
MCCALLA: Andrew, 120, 127
MCCARTY: Jeremiah, 34, 35
MCCLEARY: Samuel, 123
MCCLEYEA: Henry, 122
MCCLURE: John, 23, 37; Thomas, 110, 121; William, 41, 61, 86, 88, 97
MCCOLLOUGH/MCCULLOUGH: William, 72, 76, 81, 82, 84, 126
MCCONNELL: James, 81
MCCORMACK: Hugh, 44
MCCOY: Edward, 111
MCDANIEL: James, 59, 60, 104, 122
MCELYARY: Henry, 122
MCGUIRE: Thomas, 8; William, 8, 17, 66, 100
MCHANEY: James, 102
MCHUGHS: Moses, 25
MCKAY: Alexander, 47, 61, 74
MCKINLEY: Andrew, 56, 64
MCKINNEY: James, 106; Joseph, 69, 106, 107, 125
MCKINSY: John, 78; Nancy, 78
MCLEAN/MCCLANE: John, 76, 81, 82, 86, 98, 99, 118
MCLEOD'S FORT, 77
MCMAHAN: James, 41; John, 12, 15, 41, 49
MCMANUS/MCMANAS: James, 11, 23, 28, 41, 86, 103
MCMULLEN: Alexander, 124; John, 87, 124
MCNEALY/MCNEELY: David, 14; Hannah, 29; Jam, 14; James, 3, 14, 18, 26, 29, 32, 34, 44, 49, 53; Michael, 5, 8, 11, 14, 18, 19, 23, 25, 26, 29, 31, 32, 36, 41, 46, 48, 49, 54, 60, 63, 67, 72, 86, 92, 112, 115, 118, 125-127, 130
MCNUTT: Francis, 93, 97, 114, 130, 131; James, 81, 93, 115, 119, 120, 129-132
MCQUEEN: James, 88; John, 88; Joseph, 91; Joshua, 42, 55, 129; Margaret, 91
MCWHORTER: James, 56
MCWILLIAMS: David, 113; John, 109, 121
MADDEN: Elizabeth, 128; George, 128
MANIER/MANIRE: John, 30, 34, 47, 89, 125
MANN: John, 55, 58, 64, 68; William, 46
MARTIN: Azariah, 30, 35, 43, 44, 59, 70, 82, 87, 90, 97, 107, 113,

MARTIN (cont.): 119, 128; James, 5, 39, 47, 48, 57-59, 67, 72, 74, 82, 89, 99, 105, 109, 114, 118, 127, 129; John, 41, 44, 48, 57-59, 65-67, 72, 74, 90, 97, 107, 120, 124

MASON: Elizabeth, 76, 78; James, 13, 23, 37, 47, 76, 78, 131; William, 99

MASSIE/MASSEY, 54: David, 114, 132; Harris, 30, 49, 50, 62, 82, 85, 87, 90, 103, 104, 107, 110, 111, 114, 115, 119, 127, 128; Thomas, 108, 119

MASTERSON: Richard, 11, 15, 37

MATHEWS: James, 65, 90, 107; John, 27, 57, 72, 74, 77, 114; Robert, 77; William, 58, 64, 68

MAUPIN: Cornelius, 84

MAXFIELD: David, 16; John, 11; Thomas, 11

MAXWELL: Alexander, 65, 66; Baziel, 55, 58, 118, 127; David, 16, 23, 31, 78; David D., 63; John, 22, 31, 36, 41, 79, 86; Mary, 23, 63; Thomas, 84, 96, 128

MAY: Jesse, 65, 106, 114, 115, 129

MERRITT/MERIT: Joseph, 42, 47, 57, 68, 69, 72, 80, 87; Marget, 23; Stephen, 16, 23, 47, 91, 118

MIDDLETON: Walter, 118, 128

MILFORD, 111: plan of, 97; public lands, 93; store at, 52; survey of, 38, 40

MILL: Richard, 70

MILLER: Andrew, 31, 32, 61, 71, 93, 115; George, 14; Jacob, 38, 92; John, 6, 9, 10, 14, 16, 18, 19, 22, 24, 27, 31, 46, 50-52, 69, 72, 76, 82-84, 94, 116, 131; Nancy, 105, 125; William, 5, 46, 49, 61, 65, 66, 81, 83, 94, 105, 125, 131, 132

MILLS (water): Adams', 110; Carpenter & Woods, 38, 100, 104; Cochran's, 81, 85; Ham's, 4, 8, 16, 19, 55, 65, 78; Lewis', 92, 94, 98, 103; Ray's, 40; Titus', 24

MISE/MIZE: Isaac, 36, 87

MITCHELL: John, 33, 43, 44, 48, 55, 56, 58, 59, 66-69, 77, 80, 109, 114, 119

MOBERLY/MOBLEY: Benjamin, 91; Edward, 91; John, 91, 118

MONTGOMERY: James, 118; John, 101; Joseph, 76; Thomas, 101, 112, 121; William, 72, 112

MOORE: Arthur, 64, 66, 68; David, 128; James, 68; John, 48, 95, 127, 128; Joseph, 48, 55, 67, 106; Luke, 56, 60, 66, 68, 81, 88, 97, 106, 113; Robert, 36, 41, 46, 47, 49, 59, 74, 76, 89, 97, 103; William, 9, 30, 37, 41, 49, 58, 64, 68, 71, 120, 126; William Jr., 81

MORGAN: John, 48; Ralph, 15, 17, 19, 43, 58, 67, 73

MORRISON: Thomas, 72; William, 2, 9, 11, 13, 16, 22, 47, 53, 54, 57, 61, 67, 74, 82, 96, 107

MORROW: Samuel, 93, 121, 129, 130
MORTON: Benjamin, 61, 95; John, 91; Sarah, 91
MOSS: Edward, 35, 37, 38, 43, 44
MOUNCE/MOUNTS: John, 14, 27, 37, 63; John Jr., 34; John Sr., 34
MURPHY: Zephah, 122
MURRAY: William, 41, 120, 126

N

NAGLE: Hornes, 100; Maurice, 55
NASH: Marvel, 64
NEVIL: James, 97
NEWLAND: Abraham, 12, 13, 118
NICHOLS: Daniel, 120, 126, 131
NICHOLSON/NICHESON: James, 120; John, 128, 131; William, 126
NIGHT: John, 121
NOBLE: David, 56, 58, 81, 87, 120, 127, 132
NOLAND: Henry, 126; Jesse, 42, 74, 76, 80, 82, 86, 98, 117, 127; William, 98
NORTHCUT, 66: Benjamin, 56, 60, 64, 68, 81, 88, 97, 106, 113

O

OAKLEY/OKLEY: Benjamin, 45, 65, 85, 86, 127; William, 45, 113
OFFE/EOFFE: Alexander, 49, 119; Isaac, 112
ORCHARD: John, 36; William, 75, 80, 89, 92
OREAR: William, 7, 12, 13, 17, 31, 34, 36, 37, 67, 75, 111, 112
ORR: Alexander, 43
OWDEN: Thomas, 72, 76
OWENS/OWINS: John, 23, 41
OWLEY/OWSLEY: Christopher, 10, 13, 41, 60; Elizabeth, 63; Henry, 11, 22, 26, 31, 36, 55, 86; John, 10, 13, 21, 60, 62, 63, 101; Jonathan, 58, 61, 63, 64, 68, 71, 90, 98, 99, 101, 103, 106, 115, 120, 131; Michael, 18; Peter, 22, 26, 31, 36; Rebeka, 13; Thomas, 131; William, 101
OZBURN: Mark, 66

P

PARKER, 86, 87: Edward, 36, 83; Jeremiah, 42, 75, 80, 83
PARKHAM: Thomas, 58, 103, 125
PARREL/PERREL: William, 83, 87
PASLEY: Thomas, 100, 115, 119, 126
PATTEN/PATTON/PATTERN: Isaac, 66; Jacob, 83, 119; John, 130; Joseph, 23; William, 93
PATTERSON: John, 76; Matthew, 131
PATTIE: John, 23
PATTISON: Jacob, 108
PAWLING: William, 57
PEMBERTON: Bennett, 2, 28, 29, 40, 63, 121; Bent, 8, 10; Captain, 6, 7, 19
PEPPERS: Prudence, 8
PERKINS/PURKINS: Thomas, 37; William, 16

PERRY: Jeremiah, 47, 57, 65, 68, 72, 88, 97, 98, 106, 107, 114, 129
PERSONS: John, 90
PEYTON: Dorothy, 78; Yelverton, 131
PHELPS: Cary, 64-66, 71, 102, 114; John, 15, 54, 55, 58, 64, 76, 80, 92, 96, 97, 102, 129; John Jr., 26, 64; Joseph, 96, 122, 127; Josiah, 46
PHILIPS: Philip, 28, 49, 54, 57
PIPER: Prudence, 8
PITMAN: Dorotha, 70; John, 25, 47, 55, 57, 58, 64, 70, 72, 78, 80, 83, 84, 86, 90, 96, 117; Joseph, 67
PLATT: Ebenezer S., 22
POE: William, 37, 70
POLLARD: Anne, 93; William, 30, 67, 68, 73, 79, 91, 93, 113
POOR: overseers of, 60
PORTWOOD: Page, 46, 49, 82, 92, 93, 111, 118
POWEL: William, 65
PRATER/PRATOR/PRAYTOR: Edward, 29; John, 29, 41, 104, 116; William, 105
PREACHERS, 7, 45, 47, 79, 101
PROCTOR: Benjamin, 41, 48, 57, 63, 68, 126; Joseph, 63, 82, 106, 107, 110, 111; Nicholas, 26, 33, 44, 48, 58, 59, 64, 68, 69, 75, 81, 110, 111, 130; Rachel, 33; Rubin, 11, 14
PROVINCE: John, 126
PRUITT: Anthony, 87; Isham, 87

PRYER: Paton, 100
PULLINS/PULLENS/POLLINS: Lofty, 11, 16, 46, 61, 79, 86, 118, 119
PURNEL: William, 87
PURSEL/PURSLEY/PERSLEY: Benjamin, 84, 92, 110, 117

Q

QUINN: Benjamin, 91; Franky, 91

R

RAPERDAN: Frederick, 66, 75, 80, 90, 97, 106
RAY: Joseph, 2, 16, 18, 23, 40, 44
RAYBURN: Robert, 30
REDMAN: George, 82, 86, 98
REED/REID: Alexander, 4, 25, 35, 44, 55, 60, 65, 70, 73, 79, 81, 90, 91, 93, 105-107, 110, 111, 114, 115, 118, 119, 127; James, 89, 107; John, 58, 73, 86, 88, 93, 97, 101, 105
REPHEART: Jacob, 113
REYNOLDS/RANNELLS/RUNNALLS: Charles, 111; Richard, 4, 27, 41, 53, 70, 72, 74, 77, 79, 105, 115, 129; Thomas, 24, 64, 67, 68, 71, 75, 82, 98, 103, 118, 129
RICE, 48: David, 41; Samuel, 2, 6, 10, 19, 36, 45, 47, 48, 55, 62, 64, 66, 68, 74, 82, 87, 89, 128
RICKETT: William, 71
RIDDLE: Moses, 86, 96
RIDLEY: Bromfield, 55, 60

Index

ROBARDS: Jesse, 64; Thomas, 90, 98, 101, 103
ROBERTS: Benett, 55, 67; John, 132; Thomas, 86; William, 43
ROBERTSON, 43: James, 2, 3, 5, 11, 26, 32, 34, 37, 44, 49, 85, 90, 105, 130; Sarah, 34, 70, 78; William, 26, 34, 37, 38, 43, 44, 46, 49, 55, 58, 66, 67, 70, 78, 81, 122, 127, 130
ROBINSON: James, 2, 3, 32, 34, 35, 85, 90, 130; James Jr., 96; James Sr., 96; Payton, 131; William, 23, 26, 66, 88, 122
RODES/ROADS: R., 20; Robert, 4, 7, 9, 10, 15, 18, 29, 31, 39, 40, 45, 47, 69, 72, 80, 88, 94, 95, 99, 125, 127, 131
ROGERS/RODGERS: Anthony, 37, 55, 58, 90, 97, 101, 102, 106, 116, 120, 128, 131; John, 125
ROLLS: Hardy, 90, 106, 131
ROSS: Ambrose, 11, 16, 22, 23, 26, 31, 41, 53, 118; Hugh, 10, 11, 14, 15, 18, 21, 23, 25, 30, 32, 37, 41, 43, 48, 53, 57, 58, 63, 82, 86, 98, 101, 103, 124; James, 82
ROWLAND: Mary, 121
RUSH: John, 85
RUSSELL: Edward, 120

S

SADERS: John, 19
SANDERS: John, 15, 17, 19; Thomas, 98
SAPPINGTON/SAPATON: Hartley, 102; James, 102; Jemima, 102; John, 17, 22, 46, 84, 86, 99, 100, 102, 117, 130; Joseph, 96
SAWYERS: John, 108
SCOTT: James, 96; Joseph, 3, 5, 22, 26, 30, 31, 36, 44, 47, 49, 55-57, 72, 75, 81, 84, 86, 92, 104, 127, 131; Matthew, 2, 5, 6, 85, 92, 100, 131
SEARCY: Asa, 80, 89, 103, 122, 128, 130, 131; Bennett, 60, 62; Charles, 29, 55; Lucy, 90, 101, 103; Reubin, 47, 55, 60, 103, 127
SHACKELFORD: Edward, 37; James, 64, 98, 101, 103, 115, 131; Samuel, Jr., 116; Samuel, 118, 121
SHELTON: David, 61, 74; Thomas, 6, 9, 24, 26, 30, 33, 84, 89
SHERIFF: appointment of, 40, 51, 91, 112
SHIP: John, 60
SHOEMAKER: Solomon, 106, 114, 115
SHORT: Joel, 127
SIMMONS: Charles, 64
SIMPSON/SIMSON: Charles, 57, 68; William, 66, 75, 80, 90, 97, 106
SIMS: Elizabeth, 121; Mathew, 106, 107, 121; Randol, 106
SINCLAIR: Alexander, 34, 121
SINGLETON: Richard, 2, 13
SLAVES: Fanny, 40; Jacob, 26; Jane, 40
SLAVIN: John, 104

SMALL: Samuel, 118; William, 61, 90
SMITH: Bennett, 69, 72; Caleb, 12; Carr, 39, 111; Francis, 71; George, 76, 93; James, 15, 43, 47, 55, 99, 108; John, 17, 19, 34, 121; Reuben, 127; Richard, 129; William, 106
SNODDY: John, 1, 4, 6, 7, 10, 22, 33, 40, 50, 51, 60, 62, 69, 71, 77, 78, 85, 103, 110, 112
SOUTH: John, 4, 20, 37, 46, 49, 52, 54, 58, 59, 73, 92, 94, 99, 101-103, 109, 111, 115, 129, 132; John Sr., 43; Samuel, 2, 9, 43, 45, 61, 109, 122; Weldon, 37, 44, 45, 49, 56, 65, 118; William, 132; Zedikiah, 59
SOUTHERLAND/SUTHERLAND: David, 126; Thomas, 69, 75, 80, 81, 88, 93, 118; William, 64, 68, 82, 90
SPRING, 90
SPROWL: William, 36, 44, 49, 56
STAFFORD: William, 37
STAGNER: Barney, 54, 55, 67, 68, 75, 81, 88, 102, 104, 113-115, 128
STAMPER: Joshua, 92, 94
STARNES/STARNS/STEARNS: Adam, 26, 57; Captain, 8, 19; Elizabeth, 10; Jacob, 2, 8, 10, 43, 72, 76, 92, 118; John, 119
STEEL: John, 106, 107, 129
STEPHENS/STEVENS: Abraham, 110; Thomas, 36, 85

STEPHENSON, 75: Edward, 11, 13, 21, 22, 29, 53, 61, 75, 112; Elizabeth, 6, 8, 99, 100, 112; James, 5, 6, 8, 10, 13, 16, 24, 55, 58, 59, 96, 106, 107, 114, 121, 122, 130, 131; John, 116
STEPP: John, 60, 100
STEWART/STUART: William, 112, 129
STIVERS: Reubin, 87
STONE: Valentine, 43, 92, 94, 105
STURGIS: James A., 35
SURVEYOR: appointment of, 6
SURVEYS RECORDED, 40
SYDBOTTOM: John, 67

T

TALBOT: Haile, 6, 9, 15, 21, 24, 36, 40, 49, 50, 60, 78, 80, 88, 125
TANNER: David, 113; John, 4, 7, 17, 42, 71, 98, 101, 115, 119, 126, 131, 132; Mary, 113; Rachel, 42, 71
TAVERN: license for, 55
TAYLOR: Ann, 20; Edward, 65, 70, 93, 112; Frances, 39; Peter, 11, 20, 22, 26, 36, 43, 44, 55, 76, 79, 87, 96, 105, 106, 112, 113, 116, 118, 129
TERRILL/TARIL/TERREL: Edmund, 5, 23, 24, 37, 40, 67, 104; Judy, 23; Reubin, 58; Robert, 41; William, 66, 86
TETER: George, 56, 63, 65, 81, 86; George, Jr., 53; George, Sr., 53; Samuel, 57, 65, 70, 92

TEVIS: Robert, 82
THOMAS: William, 44, 49
THOMPSON: Closs, 91, 104; Henry, 129; James, 1, 116; John, 43; Lawrence, 122
THORP: Dotson, 42, 65, 132
THREADGILE: William, 71
TILLEY/TILLY: James, 35, 45; James Jr., 35; Jane, 45; Patsey, 45
TIPTON: Thomas, 4, 23, 25, 65
TITSWORTH: Benjamin, 109
TITUS: Joseph, 20, 24, 54, 57, 58, 66, 80, 81, 99, 108
TODD: Robert, 56, 81, 87; Thomas, 14, 82, 114, 129
TOMPKINS/THOMPKINS: Giles, 67, 70
TOWNS: Oswell/Oswald, 2, 15, 109, 121
TUCKER, 49, 57: Enoch, 66
TUDER: John, 15
TUNSTALL: Richard, 87, 94, 105, 109
TURNER: Edward, 14, 27, 28, 36, 41, 43, 55, 62, 63, 70, 73, 74, 76, 86, 99, 104, 118, 121, 132; James, 63; John, 4, 28, 99; Joseph, 73; Michael, 125; Thomas, 6, 70, 122
TURNEY: Michael, 125
TURPIN/TURPEN: Elizabeth, 74, 76, 78; Martin, 87; Nathan, 100; Solomon, 74, 76; William, 9, 20, 36, 40, 43, 100, 117, 126

V
VANCLEAVE: William, 70
VANNOY: Andrew, 54
VAUGHN/VON: James, 58, 97, 101, 102, 128
VIVION: John, 23

W
WALKER: Asaph, 53, 61; James, 92, 93; Matthew, 90, 101, 103; Richard, 22, 31, 32, 34, 36, 46, 73, 102, 129; Stephen, 101, 102
WALLACE: Michael, 91, 98, 105, 125; William, 53, 63, 84, 128, 131
WALTON: Matthew, 33
WAREHOUSE: Boonsborough, 46, 47, 118; inspectors at, 46, 54, 73, 79; land surveyed for, 99; plans for, 45, 88; public, 45; scales at, 80, 113; tobacco at, 100, 132
WARREN: John, 82, 86, 98, 101, 103; Thomas, 2, 10, 36, 43, 48, 50, 59, 66, 114
WATSON: Evan, 96, 114, 115, 119, 129; Jesse, 8, 95, 96; John, 91; Milley, 96; Thomas, 96; William, 120
WELCH: Nicholas, 116, 125; Thomas, 43, 49, 57, 60, 63, 64, 68, 71, 125; Zachariah, 125
WELDON, 71: John, 82, 90, 97, 107, 109, 114, 119, 130; Joseph, 53, 69, 82, 86, 87, 90, 107, 114, 119, 128; Phebe, 74

WELLS: David, 73, 96, 100, 128; Henry, 66
WEST: Jeremiah, 57; William, 94, 126
WHEELER: Benjamin, 93, 96, 121
WHITE: Aquilla, 2, 15, 43, 47, 54, 55, 81, 115, 119; James, 89; John, 5, 16, 17, 55, 56, 70, 73, 82, 96, 100, 104; Nicholas, 121; Stephen, 127, 132; Thomas, 81, 84
WILBURN: Thomas, 79; Zachariah, 125
WILCOCKS: David, 70, 92
WILEY: Andrew, 131
WILKERSON: John, 73, 92, 105; William, 113
WILKINSON: James, 111; John, 22, 105; William, 113
WILLIAMS: Benjamin, 58, 68, 71, 75; Daniel, 18, 122; Edmund, 104; Edward, 35, 37, 41, 42, 55, 59, 65, 69, 72, 79, 82, 88, 96, 104, 112, 120, 122; Elizabeth, 107; Francis, 109; Isaac, 30, 65, 86, 91, 109, 110; John, 55, 60; Philip, 16, 19, 53, 61, 116; William, 6, 7, 30, 39, 42, 66, 70, 92, 104, 118, 130
WILLIAMSON: Thomas, 45
WILLIS: Drury, 130; Elizabeth, 94, 95; Sherod, 116
WILMORE: Thomas, 79
WILSON: Jesse, 8; John, 21, 36, 39, 45, 81, 109, 125
WOLFSCALE: George, 61, 74, 129; Joseph, 128; William, 131
WOODARD: Benjamin, 11, 14
WOODRUFF/WOODROOF/WOODROUGH, 7, 8: David, 116; John, 4, 38, 65, 70, 73
WOODS, 90: Abigail, 122; Abner, 15; Adam, 2, 6, 10, 94, 95, 100, 108; Andrew, 37, 47, 63, 70; Archibald, 1, 3, 4, 6-8, 10, 13-15, 20, 24, 26, 33, 36, 38-40, 42, 51, 69, 70, 77, 78, 84, 92, 94, 96, 103, 104, 107, 111, 125, 128; John, 6, 53, 63, 77, 86, 114, 122, 131; Michael, 27; Mourning, 125; Peter, 2, 8, 38, 40, 66, 79; Robert, 94; Samuel, 3, 5, 7, 9, 34, 75, 77, 79, 86, 89, 127; William, 66, 90, 114
WOODS' STATION, 63, 70, 87, 92
WOOLEY/WOLEY/WOOLY: See also Owley, .; Christopher, 41; Henry, 22, 55, 77; John, 21; Peter, 22, 41
WRIGS: Bathuel, 128
WYCOFF: William, 37

Y

YANCY: Robert, 131
YATER: Henry, 64
YATES: John, 127
YOCUM: George, 34, 60
YOUNG: John, 116; William, 12, 37, 112, 119

www.ingramcontent.com/pod-product-compliance
Lightning Source LLC
Chambersburg PA
CBHW050823160426
43192CB00010B/1877